D1230481

Poetics of Children's Literature

Zohar Shavit

POETICS
OF CHILDREN'S
LITERATURE

The University of Georgia Press
Athens and London

© 1986 by the University of Georgia Press
Athens, Georgia 30602

Designed by Sandra Strother Hudson
Set in Mergenthaler ten on twelve digital Ehrhardt
The paper in this book meets the guidelines for
permanence and durability of the Committee on
Production Guidelines for Book Longevity of the
Council on Library Resources.

Printed in the United States of America

89 88 87 86   4 3 2 1

Library of Congress Cataloging in Publication Data

Shavit, Zohar.
Poetics of children's literature.

Bibliography: p.
Includes index.
1. Children's literature—History and criticism.
I. Title.
PN1009.A1S38   1986   809'.89282   85-1110
ISBN 0-8203-0790-4

Chapter 1 of this book first appeared in a slightly different
form in the *Journal of Research and Development in
Education* (Spring 1983). Chapters 3 and 5 originally
were published in *Poetics Today* (Spring 1980;
Summer–Autumn 1984).

IN MEMORY OF MICHAL,

My Good Fairy

Contents

Preface

Children's literature will be discussed here not within the traditional pedagogic or educational frame of reference, but rather within that of poetics. Only a short time ago, children's literature was not even considered a legitimate field of research in the academic world. Scholars hardly regarded it as a proper subject for their work, and if they did, they were most often concerned solely with its pedagogic and educational value and not with its existence as a literary phenomenon. This tendency developed mainly as the result of two factors: first, the cultural conception of childhood in society and the attitude toward children's literature resulting from it; and secondly, the traditional evaluative criteria for the selection of objects for research.

As a result of society's concept of childhood, children's literature, unlike adult literature, was considered an important vehicle for achieving certain aims in the education of children. This belief, however, meant that children's literature could not be accepted by highbrow society as having a status equal to that of adult literature; consequently, children's literature suffered from an inferior status within the literary polysystem.

As long as the main criterion for selection of subjects for research was normative and based on the text's evaluation, there was no room for research of texts that were considered inferior or of little literary merit. This is perhaps most tellingly revealed in the amount of space devoted to children's literature in various national histories of literature and culture, in encyclopedias, and in curricula of university literature departments. Without exaggerating, children's literature is almost totally ignored by such cultural institutions. Still, children's literature has not been altogether neglected by scholars and critics, since some disciplines have dealt with it, such as librarianship, education, and psychological studies. The main questions that concerned those fields were: What is a good book for a child? What is the influence of a book on a child? How can it contribute to the child's development?

Such important questions, essential as they may be for those fields, have undoubtedly limited the scope of research to a large extent. In order to free research of these limitations and allow room for new and different questions, two drastic changes must take place in the research of children's literature. First, scholars must indicate their readiness to accept children's literature as a legitimate field of research; secondly, they must be ready to regard children's literature as literature per se, that is, to regard it as a part of the literary system, which does not mean, of course, that the evaluation of the texts must change as well.

These needed changes have already begun to occur in the hitherto closed field of literary research. During the last ten years or so, new interest has arisen in the field of children's literature, and important work has been done, notably in the compilation of national histories of children's literature. Unfortunately, the fact that a new field of research is in the process of developing has not been fully exploited by scholars. Instead of applying the latest achievements in literary scholarship (in both the Eastern and Western worlds) to this new field, most scholars have preferred to study children's literature strictly within the context of traditional and overworn questions.

In this study I relate this newly developed field to the latest achievements of poetics and semiotics, areas that are quite new to the English-speaking world. I believe that the time has arrived to extricate children's literature from the narrow boundaries of the past and to place it in the foreground of literary scholarship, facing the future.

Hence, the point of departure in my study is the assumption that children's literature is part of the literary polysystem, that it is a member of a stratified system in which the position of each member is determined by socioliterary constraints. Thus, it is an integral part of society's cultural life, and only as such, should it be analyzed. This conceptual change in the understanding of children's literature requires the total exclusion of normative or ideological questions (such as the contribution of a certain book to the child's welfare); moreover, it challenges the scholar to raise new and previously undiscussed questions. With the help of these questions, I explore not only the inherent nature of children's literature, but also general patterns of behavior in the literary polysystem, as well as the particular cultural context in which children's literature has developed.

The study of both literature and culture can greatly benefit from an in-depth examination of children's literature, for children's literature, much more so than adult literature, is the product of constraints imposed on it by several cultural systems, such as the educational, the ideological, and so on. Nevertheless, my approach to children's literature, while aiming at an improved understanding of its structures and patterns, does not aim to change the status of children's literature within the literary polysystem; my primary aim is simply to engender a better comprehension of this status and its implications.

While I have deliberately avoided traditional evaluative questions in this study, I have tried to raise new ones concerning the relationships between cultural concepts, images, and consciousness and texts produced for children.

Thus my study endeavors on the one hand to analyze the way society's changing concepts of childhood are responsible for different texts for the child in different periods, while on the other, to examine how the cultural position of children's literature imposes certain patterns of behavior, such as a tendency to self-perpetuation, a readiness to accept only well-established models and reject new models, the need to appeal to two contradicting audiences, and others.

It is not the isolated text I am interested in, nor the cumulative history of any specific national children's literature. *The issue at stake is rather the universal structural traits and patterns common to all children's literatures,* taking into account the periods in which they occur and the different rates of their development.

This study deals with issues and not with individual texts, with historical processes and not with chronological descriptions, and finally, with structures and not with interpretations. The texts (mostly English and Hebrew) have been chosen because they exemplify the issues discussed and thus serve as the best test cases. The issues appear to be cardinal as well as recurrent in the field; thus, their study addresses itself not only to scholars of children's literature, but also to those concerned with semiotics, poetics, and the history of culture. Therefore, my purpose here is two-fold: to contribute to the research of semiotics and to open a new and fruitful direction in the study of children's literature.

Department of Poetics and Comparative Literature
Tel Aviv University
IYL, Munich

April 1983

Acknowledgments

 With great pleasure I wish to thank colleagues and institutions who have helped me in the writing of this book.

To Professor Susan Stewart of Temple University, who was the best reader one could dream of, whose consistent encouragement was indispensable, and whose careful remarks were so excellent that her contribution to the book cannot be exaggerated.

To Professor Itamar Even-Zohar, Tel Aviv University, to whose work in the field of poetics and semiotics I am greatly indebted; to John McGuigan, who actually initiated this work and very patiently encouraged me in its writing; to Ramon Maayan-Rosen, David Myers, and Debbie Winter, my marvelous editors; to Ms. Erika von Engebrechten, the librarian of the International Youth Library, who made my stay there so fruitful; to the International Youth Library of Munich, whose scholarship gave me time and peace for research and writing. To the Betty and Walter Artzt Chair for History of Poetry and Literature and to the Porter Institute for Poetics and Semiotics for their support, and to the secretary of the Institute, Sharon Himmelfarb, who was always willing to help.

And last, but not least, to my children, Noga and Uriya, who despite my work are still enthusiastic readers of children's books, and my newborn, Avner, who hopefully will be one; and to my husband, Yaacov Shavit, who patiently shared with me the long gestation period of this book, but waited like a devoted father until delivery was over.

Part One

STATE OF THE SYSTEM

Chapter One

The Notion of Childhood
and Texts for the Child

 Today it is difficult to imagine the book industry without its huge output of children's books. The mass production of children's books is taken for granted as a prominent and indispensable part of publishing activity. The twentieth-century cultural (and conceptual) obsession with the physical, mental, and sexual problems of childhood is also readily accepted. Society views childhood as the most important period of life and tends to account for most of adult behavior on the basis of childhood experience. Society is so used to its understanding of what childhood is, as well as to the existence of books for children, that it forgets that both concepts, childhood and books for children, are relatively new phenomena; that is, society's present view of childhood is far removed from that which was held only two centuries ago. Moreover, children's literature began to develop only after adult literature had become a well-established institution. Books specifically for children were seldom written until the eighteenth century, and the whole industry of children's books began to flourish only in the second half of the nineteenth century.

The connection between these two facts is neither random nor insignificant, but rather the creation of the notion of childhood was an indispensable precondition for the production of children's books and determined to a large extent the development and options of development for children's literature. This chapter will discuss how and when this process took place.

Before children's literature could begin to develop, a total reform in the notion of childhood was required, a reform that was described in the pioneering and well-known work of Philippe Ariès (1962) and

3

in recent research (see Weber-Kellermann 1979, Plessen and von Zahn 1979). Before this reform surfaced in the nineteenth century, society held a different view of childhood, which began to change during the seventeenth century. Before this, before children's needs gained recognition and legitimation as *distinct and different from adults'*, children's literature could not have existed. As Townsend states: "Before there could be children's books, there had to be children—children, that is, who were accepted as beings with their own particular needs and interests, not only as miniature men and women" (Townsend 1977, 17).

The View of Childhood Until the Seventeenth Century: From Unity to Polarity

I do not intend to survey Ariès's work nor that of his followers in this study, but rather to elaborate on the aforementioned connection between the development of the notion of childhood and that of children's literature. Yet, in order to trace this connection, one of Ariès's most important contentions (an uncontradicted one, despite quite a few attempts to dispute it; see, for instance, deMause 1975), must be accepted as a basic premise.

Before discussing Ariès's thesis, a short digression must be made. This book basically accepts his thesis and even takes his description of the evolution of the notion of the child as its beginning point. However, since his thesis is so comprehensive, certain modifications and a few reformulations are required. For instance, Ariès's theory is strongly built upon the French case. When other cases are examined (Germany, England) they are not parallel either in time or in the way the same historical phenomena evolved. Nevertheless, it can still be argued that the same process of development of the notion of the child occurred throughout Western Europe. When the development of the notion of the child is examined, one can consistently discern how around the beginning of the sevententh century (in some cases earlier, in some later), a totally new understanding of "childhood" developed, which consistently created two new cultural institutions: a new system of education, the school system, and a new readership that produced an unprecedented market for children's books.

4

Hence, Ariès's basic thesis that cultural understanding of childhood has greatly changed in Western society is, in my view, indisputable. Those who try to challenge it, especially the recent study of Pollock (1983), simply do not understand either the implications of his study or the mechanism of historical developments and historical changes. Attacking Ariès's thesis by claiming that the same notion of childhood always existed, implies a total misunderstanding of the meaning of a new historical phenomenon.

A new historical phenomenon does not necessarily mean—in fact, it never means—that a certain element or group of elements abruptly changes overnight, or that a new phenomenon is totally new in all its components and functions. Quite the contrary, any historical change requires time before cultural consciousness has recognized it as a change, and normally, it is enough for any historical phenomenon to be considered "new" when only some of its components are changed.

In summation, to accept Ariès's thesis does not imply an absurd understanding of historical processes; it does not mean that suddenly all Europeans understood differently what a child was and what his specific needs were. It does, however, mean accepting a description of historical development that began in the seventeenth century and culminated in the nineteenth century, during which time a new understanding evolved of what childhood is and, consequently, what the needs of the child are. Ariès argued that until the seventeenth century children were not considered different from adults. It was assumed that they had no special needs, and as a result, there was neither an established educational system, nor were there any books for children.

In medieval society and in the centuries that followed, the prevailing theological approach, as well as conditions of life, left no room for the extravagance of childhood. The conceptual framework of society ignored the characteristics distinguishing a child from an adult. Of course, differences did exist, but they were simply not recognized. On the theological plane, it was believed that the cycle of life—analogous to that of nature—consisted of birth, life, and death, thus leaving no room for the stage of childhood. Moreover, the conditions of life, including a high rate of child mortality and a short life span, contributed to reinforcing the conceptual ignorance of childhood: childhood was too "fragile" a period and the children that survived it had to leave childhood early and enter manhood because the life span was so short. Accordingly, once the child left his swaddling, he was considered an integral part of adult society, sharing adult dress, work, and leisure. However, by the beginning of the seventeenth century, this unity in the world of the adult and the child began to undergo polarization, resulting in a new concept of childhood.

This new concept emerged in society because of certain occurrences, among which the most important were changes in the current ideas of the time. Surprising as it may seem, they preceded the well-known changes in social conditions usually linked with the emergence of childhood, such as the Industrial Revolution, the emergence of the bourgeois class, and the drop in the child mortality rate. Undoubtedly, these things also played a role in the development of the notion of childhood; yet the changes in the ideological sphere in which a distinct view of the child began to develop came more than a century before the material changes.

For the first time, children were described as having special distinguishing characteristics, such as innocence, sweetness, and other angelic qualities. These new ideas of children, as Ariès claims, can be traced back to the late sixteenth century to religious paintings that used the child for religious purposes (to symbolize the child Jesus, Jesus and the angels, and others). Later, this iconography acquired a more decorative function (as opposed to religious) in the form of the putto. In fact, as paintings of children took on nonreligious themes and began to dominate art and iconography, the idea of childhood as an independent stage was absorbed more and more by society. These paintings expressed the special traits children were now seen as possessing. No doubt they were partly responsible for society's new awareness of children's special qualities of sweetness and innocence. These qualities led to the child gradually becoming a source of amusement and relaxation for adults, thus negating the former view of children as merely small adults. In this way, the unified world of adults and children underwent polarization. Several elements, such as toys and dress, previously shared by both adults and children, now became the child's monopoly, although usually through a process of reduction and simplification. Soon after, they also became elements with a distinguishing function, pointing to the new border between adults and children.

This new view of the child was first propagated within the family circle. In quite a short time, parents would no longer hesitate to admit the pleasure they obtained from their children. Furthermore, they would refuse to stop mollycoddling them. In a way, children were treated like pets—a constant source of amusement for adult company—which made Claude Fleury protest in the following manner: "It is as if the poor children had been made only to amuse the adults, like little dogs or little monkeys" (Ariès 1962, 131). Not long after this idea of childhood as a source of amusement came to be accepted by society, a new view that accepted the original contention of differentiation, but objected to its errant course, began to develop, especially among moralists and pedagogues within the church. They agreed that children were different from adults, but drew the conclusion that innocent children and creatures close to god should be isolated from the corrupting company of adults. Thus evolved a second notion of childhood. This notion was mainly concerned with the spiritual well-being of the child and held that children should be educated and disciplined; furthermore, it prescribed a new role for adults in which they were responsible for the spiritual well-being of the child. In this new conceptual framework arose for the first time serious psychological interest in the child, as well as demand for an organized educational system. Children were now regarded as delicate creatures who had to be reformed and safeguarded; and the way to reform them was through education and through books issued primarily as pedagogic vehicles. Hence, the society's new perception of childhood created for the first time both the *need* and the *demand* for children's books. This second notion of the child—the educational—eventually provided the framework for canonized children's literature. That is, from its inception children's books were written with a certain idea of the child in mind; when this idea changed, the texts for children changed as well.

In the same way that people assumed a child needed different dress, toys, and games, it was also assumed that a child reader differed from the adult, both in his capacity to comprehend, as well as in his educational needs. Accordingly, it was essential that the texts produced for him should respond to his needs and capacities. Of course, the understanding of these needs and capacities was not fixed, but changed from period to period, consequently changing the character of the texts for children as well.

In order to understand how concepts of childhood determined the

7

character of the texts produced for the child, various versions of "Little Red Riding Hood" will be examined. This specific text was chosen not only because of its status as a children's classic, but because its numerous versions—written at different points in time (seventeenth, nineteenth, and twentieth centuries)—reveal most clearly the diverse ways in which childhood was perceived by society in different periods, both in assumptions about the child's capacity for comprehension and society's belief about what the child should be exposed to. The drastic changes in these perceptions during the last three centuries can be traced by following the transformation of "Little Red Riding Hood" from the "coddling" version of Perrault to the "reasoning" version of Grimm, and finally to the modern "protective" versions of the twentieth century.

A Test Case: "Little Red Riding Hood"

THE ATTITUDE TOWARD FAIRY TALES
IN THE SEVENTEENTH CENTURY

As toys and dress items were transferred to the child's world with the emergence of a new concept of childhood, so also fairy tales were gradually accepted as belonging in the child's realm and became the child's monopoly. This is not to say, of course, that before the seventeenth century children were not acquainted with fairy tales—obviously they were.[1] Before fairy tales became the monopoly of children, they were read and recounted over the centuries both by adults (even of high social class) and by the children who shared their company. But although children were acquainted with fairy tales, fairy tales were not initially considered as especially intended for them (for

---

[1] Perrault's or Grimm's texts are not "pure" oral fairy tales but rather literary products arranged by the writers to suit various purposes. Since both Grimm and Perrault were presenting literary products (see Zipes 1979b, 23–24), it seems useless to distinguish throughout the discussion between oral fairy tales and fairy tales (Volksmärchen). Yet a distinction between fairy tales and fantastic narratives must be made for our further discussion of fantasy. Fantastic narrative is regarded here as a text that, though not necessarily based on fairy-tale model, rejects realistic bias. Indeed its model for presentation of the world tries to challenge such a bias and to offer an alternative.

a similar case of transformation of genre, see Brockman's most interesting analysis of the transformation of the romance into the children's literature [Brockman 1982]).

After the middle of the seventeenth century, however, an interesting and complex change ensued, involving attitudes toward fairy tales. Highbrow society, which previously did not hesitate to admit the pleasure derived from fairy tales, began to regard them as suitable only for children and people of the lower classes, claiming that they were too simple and naive for anyone else. At the same time, a new interest arose in fairy tales, which made them a fashionable and artistic genre. This new interest was the motivation behind the creation of fairy tales based on the model of the traditional naive texts. However, an indispensable precondition was required for the "fashionable" writing of fairy tales; although they were in vogue, it was necessary for both writers and readers to assume that fairy tales were written for the lower classes and children. Thus adults of the upper classes could enjoy fairy tales only by pretending that they were addressing children.

Adults exploited the opportunity to enjoy fairy tales during the seventeenth century through the recognition of the child's culture as distinct from their own and the use of children as a source of amusement. Therefore the reading of fairy tales by highbrows was based on a silent agreement (between them and the writer) about two implied readers—the child and the highbrow adult—and on a tacit agreement about the writer's intentions, leaving much room for the writer to play between them. This sophisticated use of the special status of fairy tales can be seen in Perrault's "Little Red Riding Hood," especially in regard to the obscure identity of the writer and the ambiguity of the text.

PERRAULT AND THE CONCEALED IDENTITY OF THE WRITER

The attitude toward the culture of the child served as background, as well as motivation and legitimation, for Perrault's *Histoires ou Contes du temps passé*. Perrault published this collection of fairy tales in 1697, some of which, like "Little Red Riding Hood," were previously unknown as written texts. Perrault's collection was only one among a prolific flow of fairy tales that flooded French literature in the late seventeenth and early eighteenth centuries (others included the fairy tales of Mme. d'Aulnoy, Mlle. Lhéritier, and Mme. Jeanne le Prince de Beaumont). *Les Contes* aroused controversy from the very beginning, not only because the stories officially addressed children (and at the same time were sophisticated and ironical), but mainly because they were not signed by Perrault. *Les Contes* was attributed to his son, Pierre Darmancour, who was seventeen at the time of its writing and nineteen at the time of publication. The nature of the text and its obscure attribution raises at least two questions: First, why did the attribution of the text remain obscured? Secondly, to whom did the text really address itself?

The question of the text attribution has remained unsolved for the last three centuries, with scholars still disagreeing over the identity of the author. Despite the fact that the texts were signed by the son of Perrault, they were already attributed to Perrault in his lifetime and have been by many since then. In two of the volumes, 1 and 37, of *Le Cabinet des Fées* (a voluminous collection that indicates the popularity of fairy tales at the time), it was claimed that Perrault himself wrote the texts, though he "attributa ses contes de fées à son fils" [attributed his fairy tales to his son] (Soriano 1978, 38).[2]

Soriano claims that the book was often attributed to Perrault due to its widespread fame and the need for an attractive name. But this argument neither explains why the text was attributed to Perrault by his contemporaries before it gained worldwide recognition, nor why Perrault himself never bothered to announce his authorship, as the dispute began even in his own day: "L'Académicien savait la vérité sur cette affaire. Mais il n'a rien fait pour éliminer la doute" [The member of the French Academy knew the truth about this affair but did nothing to eliminate the doubt.] (Soriano 1978, 69). Rather, it could be claimed that the opposite is true. It seems that Perrault did his best to conceal the identity of the writer.

Perrault did not deny that he was himself a writer. He signed his own name on "La Marquise de Salusses ou la Patience de Griselidis," which was published in *Mercure Galant*, along with a note that it was read in a lecture at the French Academy (1691); his name appeared also on "Les Souhaits ridicules" (*Mercure Galant*, 1693).

[2] All translations, unless otherwise specified, are mine. I am grateful to Nitsa Ben-Ari for her help.

But at the same time, Perrault did his best to confuse the identity of the author of *Les Contes*. Among the various means Perrault used was the following: In 1696, he published a revised and enlarged version of "L'Histoire de la Marquise-Marquis de Banneville" in *Mercure Galant*. The text was published in two installments, and in the second, a long and sarcastic digression appeared, referring to the writer of "La belle au bois dormant," which was published earlier in February 1696:

—Avez-vous lu *La Belle au bois dormant?*
—Si je l'ai lue? s'ecria la petite Marquise. Je l'ai lue quatre fois et ce petit conte m'a raccommodée avec Le *Mercure galant* où j'ai été ravie de le trouver. Je n'ai encore rien vu de mieux narré; un tour fin et délicat, des expressions toutes naïves; mais je ne m'en suis point étonnée quand on m'a dit le nom de l'auteur. Il est fils de Maître et s'il n'avait pas bien de l'esprit, il faudrait qu'on l'ait changé en nourrice. (Soriano 1978, 24–25)

["Have you read *Sleeping Beauty?*" "Yes, I have," cried the little marquise. "I read it four times and this little fairy tale reconciled me to the *Mercure galant* where I was overjoyed to find it. I have never yet seen anything better told; written so fine and delicate, very naive expressions. But I was not at all astonished when I was told the name of the writer. He is the son of a master, and had he lacked inspiration, he must have had changed hands while nursing."]

Such comments by Perrault added, of course, to the mystery and the confusion regarding the attribution of the text. The author's identity was further confused by the suggested attribution of the text to Perrault's niece, Mlle. Lhéritier, as a result of the similarities between her fairy tales and Perrault's. Yet, unlike the question of the attribution, the similarity between the texts is easily explained not only because the writers were connected by family ties and spent much time together in the same literary salons, but mainly because they based their fairy tales upon the same model and shared the same literary conventions.

How did his contemporaries react to his manipulation of the writer's identity? It seems that they were not impressed by Perrault's efforts to conceal the writer's identity; this may be assumed from a survey of their letters in which Perrault is referred to, in a most matter-of-fact fashion, as the author of *Les Contes*. In one such letter, dated 23 September 1696, Dubos wrote to Bayle: "Ce même libraire [Barbin] imprime aussi *Les Contes de ma mère l'Oye* par Monsieur Perrault. Ce sont bagatelles auxquelles il s'est amusé autrefois pour réjouir ses enfants." [This same librarian prints also *Les Contes de ma mere l'oye* by Perrault. These are nonsense stories that he wrote to amuse himself and his children.] In a second letter, dated 1 March 1697, Dubos wrote: "Madame Daunoy [d'Aulnoy] ajoute un second volume aux *Contes de ma mère l'Oye* de M. Perrault" [Madame Daunoy adds a second volume to the *Contes de ma mère l'oye* of Perrault.] (Soriano 1978, 31). If this was the case, that is, if the literary circles did not doubt the text's authorship, why was it so important for Perrault to continue playing his dual game? Why did he insist upon attributing the text to his son, while at the same time deliberately confusing the issue of the attribution? The answer might lie partly in Perrault's high social status which required that he, as a distinguished member of the French Academy, could not take official responsibility for texts considered more appropriate for young people or women to write. By attributing authorship to his son, Perrault indicated that the text was intended for children, as writing for children was considered more "natural" to young people and women, according to the general custom of the times. But even more important than the need or desire to play with the question of attribution was the fact that Perrault's game was only part of a more common game underlying the acceptability of fairy tales as an upper-class source of amusement. Highbrows enjoyed the duality of the writer in the same way they enjoyed the duality of the reader, hence forcing Perrault to maintain this duality continuously.

While quite a few scholars still describe Perrault's work in terms of either a wish to depict the Nursery Tales (Soriano 1978), or, in a more sophisticated manner, as a part of the vogue of the low people's culture, more and more scholars regard it as conscious effort to adjust the oral folktale to a socialization process of the rising bourgeois class (Darnton 1984, Zipes 1983). Whatever was the real motivation for Perrault's work, most scholars seem to agree about one thing— that Perrault did change the original folktales a great deal and adjusted them to the taste of his "salon" audience. Yet Perrault's manipulation of the writer's identity alone was not enough to maintain the duality of the text. The text must also provide unmistakable evidence as to its "real" reader, the adult, and at the same time maintain the game between its two implied audiences. This was achieved mainly through the ambiguous structures of the text and through its satirical and ironical tone.

THE AMBIGUOUS STRUCTURE OF PERRAULT'S "LITTLE RED RIDING HOOD"

"Little Red Riding Hood" was not known in print until Perrault first published it in 1697. Scholars of Perrault still disagree as to whether Perrault could have based the text on oral tradition because the fairy tale's bad ending was antithetical to that tradition. However, even those who believe that the text was originally an oral tale seem to agree that Perrault only used the model of the oral tale as a basis for his text and then elaborated it. In this way, he created both a "pseudo" oral tale and a sophisticated one as well. This explains why Perrault was so careful to maintain the illusion of the oral tale, especially from a stylistic point of view. He used elements whose function was to demonstrate the "antiquity" of the text, such as "ayant *cuit* et fait *des galettes*" [she fried and made biscuits] (my italics). He also introduced elements unacceptable in written French but recognized as a child's vocabulary; these elements, such as "la bobinette" and "la chevillette," were known as purely children's language. They served not only to create the effect of a "naive oral tale," but also to signify the child's world and emphasize the official addressee of the text.

At the same time that Perrault was careful to maintain this illusion of an oral tale, he did not hesitate to break formulaic structures, in the most strategic points, as if to call attention to his manipulation of the model of an oral tale. Thus, Perrault signaled his adult reader. In this context, his use of another typical oral tale structure, that of the dialogue, is adept. Here, Perrault first creates the impression that the formula is maintained, and only then does he break it. He uses this technique in the famous dialogue between the child and "grandmother," departing from the formulaic structure in the last line only:

13

C'est pour *mieux* t'embrasser
C'est pour *mieux* courir
C'est pour *mieux* écouter
C'est pour *mieux* voir
C'est pour *te* manger.

(Perrault, Garnier 1967, 115)

[The better to kiss you with
The better to run with
The better to listen with
The better to see with
The better to eat you with.]

Perrault also broke another traditional formula, the indispensable happy ending of the oral tale. Perrault's ending is tragic—the story ends when the wolf devours the poor little girl; no rescue is suggested: "Et en disant ces mots, ce méchant Loup se jeta sur le petit chaperon rouge, et la mangea" [And in saying these words the wicked wolf jumped at Little Red Riding Hood and ate her.] (115).

Why such a drastic break? Perhaps Perrault's drastic break from the formulaic happy ending resulted from his desire to integrate satire and irony into the form of the tragic ending in order to signal the adult reader. The tragic ending indicates that the text was a satire about "gentlemen" of the town who do not hesitate to take advantage of poor naive country girls. It leads to the ironical moral, which comes as a postscript to the tale, and concludes with: "Mais hélas! qui ne sait que ces Loups doucereux, / De tous les Loups sont les plus dangereux" [But alas, who does not know that sweetish wolves are most dangerous of all wolves.] (115). This moral suggests that the wolf represents something other than a real wolf, that it stands for "toute sorte de gens" of whom naive girls should be careful if they do not wish to be hurt. The ironical interpretation of the ending by the moral negates the possibility, suggested by Soriano, that the tragic ending indicates a warning story (Soriano claims that it is a warning story, as wolves were a real danger at the time).

The text leaves no doubt as to what the wolf stands for. In addition, the theme of gentlemen who take advantage of little country girls is heightened by the erotic characterization of the girl and by the erotic bed scene. The text does not emphasize the innocence of the

14

child, but rather her beauty—"la plus jolie"; the text also suggests the color red as her symbol. And if that is not enough, the bed scene leaves little room for imagination. The wolf invites the girl to sleep with him ("viens te coucher avec moi"). The girl undresses ("Le petit chaperon rouge se déshabille, et va se mettre dans le lit") and is astonished to discover what the wolf looks like in bed ("elle fut bien étonnée de voir comment sa Mère-grand était faite en son déshabillé") [She was very astonished to see how her grandmother looked when naked.] (Garnier 1967, 114–15). All these erotic elements point to an "erotic" structure that makes no sense unless understood as a satire about a girl seduced by a gentleman, rather than as a story about a little girl devoured by a wolf.

Hence, Perrault manipulated the oral tale through its formula, style, and structure in an intentionally ambiguous manner. What was the basis for such manipulation?

THE AMBIGUITY OF THE TEXT

The ambiguous nature of the text was primarily intended to satisfy both its official and unofficial readers. It enabled Perrault to use the status of fairy tales as texts for children, addressing them officially to children as the main consumers, while at the same time using the notion of the child as a source of amusement to allow adults (mainly highbrows) to enjoy the text, too. In this way, irony and satire signaled the highbrow adult, while the formulaic structures signaled the child reader.

In fact, strong evidence that the highbrows were not just fond of the text exists: ". . . mais l'élite leur réserve une sorte de mépris amusé" [but the elite reserves for them a sort of amused scorn] (Soriano 1978, 39). It even became the habit of salon culture to read fairy tales aloud, despite their being considered childish, naive, and amusing:

> A feature of these salons, male and female alike, was the reading aloud of *pasquinades, vaudevilles, sonnets à bouts-rimés*, and similar short pieces; and the Comtesse d'Aulnoy seems to have introduced the telling of fairy-stories in the female salons. The idea caught on and became the rage. The fashion eventually extended to the male writers. . . .

The curious point to be taken is that the stories were devised, or adapted from ancient originals, for the amusement not of children but of adults. The consequence is that, although the characters and the background belong superficially to fairy-tales, most of them are much too sophisticated for children. (Muir 1969, 36)

Like his contemporary and relative, Mlle. Lhéritier, Perrault probably wrote texts also for the amusement of his friends. The following description of Mlle. Lhéritier holds true for Perrault as well: "Mlle. Lhéritier écrit pour l'amusement des ses amis et tous ses écrits portent l'empreinte de son 'esprit salonnier' " [Mlle. Lhéritier writes for the amusement of her friends and all her writing bears the stamp of the salon spirit.] (Soriano 1978, 65).

To summarize, the notion of the child in Perrault's time served as background for *Les Contes* and as an indispensable condition for the text's acceptance by highbrow adults. Once the child was perceived differently by society and was no longer considered a source for amusement, however, texts for children changed, as did the way in which the child was characterized in those texts. This is true for all texts produced for children since the eighteenth century. It is also true for versions of "Little Red Riding Hood" that underwent various changes, culminating in Grimm's "Rotkäppchen," which itself was followed by many modern adaptations.

DIFFERENCES BETWEEN PERRAULT'S AND GRIMM'S VERSIONS

Research into folktales has granted considerable space to the dispute over the connection between *Les Contes* and the similar texts gathered by the Brothers Grimm in their *Kinder und Hausmärchen.* Scholars disagree both over the origin and the "originality" of Grimm's texts and account for similarities between Perrault and Grimm on the basis of different grounds. Some present a historical-geographical explanation, while others prefer one based on cultural relationships (Bolte and Polívka 1963) or on cultural transformation (Velten 1930). Other scholars deny any direct connection between Perrault and Grimm but claim a mediated relation through Tieck, to whom Brothers Grimm referred in their notes on "Rotkäppchen": "Bei Perrault chaperon rouge, wonach Tieck's anmuthige Bearbeitung in den romantischen Dichtungen . . ." [In Perrault's "Little Red Riding Hood," according to Tieck's charming adaptation in the romantic manner] (Grimm, Reclam 1980, Band 3, 59). Without entering into this endless dispute, my contention here is that the relation between the two versions can be illuminated from the perspective of the different prevalent notions of childhood in each period. Needless to say, this sort of explanation does not deny the results of previous research as irrelevant or inadequate, but rather illuminates the relationship between the two versions from an additional aspect.

As Ariès claims, the notion of childhood has drastically changed from the seventeenth century to the nineteenth century. In the hundred years that passed between Perrault and Grimm, the "coddling" attitude had become a very different "reasoning" attitude. This change in the concept of childhood attributed great importance to something previously unheard of—the education of the child. As a result, an educational system, based on this new conception, began to develop. The needs and demands of this educational system largely determined the character of texts written for children in two respects at least: in regard to the child's capacity to realize the text; and even more importantly, in regard to the text's obligations toward the child, reflecting the desire on the part of adults that children should gain something for their spiritual welfare from the text. Those texts, therefore, were the direct result of the way childhood was perceived by society—hence, the earlier "coddling" version of Perrault and a century later the very different "reasoning" version of Grimm.

THE DIFFERENT TONES AND ENDINGS

As has been noted by many scholars, the most obvious differences between Perrault's and Grimm's versions lie in the tones of the texts (ironical versus naive) and in the endings (tragic versus happy). The difference in tone appears to be the result of the different intentions of each writer. Perrault addressed the highbrows with satire. Yet, while he masked the satire for his official readers by employing traditional structures, he unveiled it by the ironical tone for the unofficial reader. The Brothers Grimm, on the other hand, tried to depict the tone of the narrator as naive, a technique considered essential for the "authenticity" of the text. As was claimed, the irony and satire effects of Perrault's text are mainly achieved by his play between the text and its moral. It should also be noted, however, that from the very beginning Perrault's narrator takes an ironical position, as if to warn the reader not to take him too seriously; a text that opens with "sa mère en était folle et sa mère-grand plus folle encore" [her mother was crazy about her, and her grandmother even crazier] simply cannot be taken seriously. Brothers Grimm, on the other hand, achieved the effect of "naivety" by stylistic "simplicity" (short sentences, simple dialogue, limited lexicon). This stylistic simplicity is justified by adapting the narration to the child's point of view and presenting part of the discourse through her eyes. This is most evident when the child is rescued by the hunter: she does not realize how dangerous it was (nor does the text indicate so in any way), but "merely" declares how frightful the darkness in the wolf's belly was! The text further depicted the childish tone by using the exclamation word "ach": "Ach, wie war ich erschrocken, wie war's so dunkel in dem wolf seinem Leib!" [Ah, how shocked I was. How dark it was in the wolf's belly!] (Grimm, Reclam 1980, 159). This device was justified by Brothers Grimm in their foreword to *Kinder und Hausmärchen*, where the new image of childhood is presented. In this foreword, Brothers Grimm emphasized the child's pureness and genuine capacity to see the world in a special way—a new image of the child common to the Brothers Grimm and to their nineteenth-century contemporaries:

> Darum geht innerlich durch diese Dichtungen jene Reinheit, um derentwillen uns Kinder so wunderbar und selig erscheinen: sie haben gleichsam dieselben blaulichweissen makellosen glänzenden Augen, die nicht mehr wachsen können, während sie andern Glieder noch zart, schwach und zum Dienste der Erde ungeschickt sind. (Grimm, Reclam 1980, Band 1, 16)

> [These paragraphs express this purity that makes our children appear so wonderful and blessed; they all have these blue-white faultless bright eyes, that can no longer grow while other members of their body are still so soft, weak and still unprepared for the service of the earth.]

However, what has primarily attracted the attention of scholars is the very different endings of the two versions. In Perrault's version the story ends when the child is devoured by the wolf, while Grimm's version offers two alternative endings, in both of which the child is rescued. In the first ending, the child is punished—grandmother and child are devoured—and only later rescued when the wolf is killed; in the second, the wolf is killed by drowning without hurting the child at all (on the "educational" message of the second ending, see my later discussion). Why, then, was the happy ending needed?

Researchers of fairy tales are still debating the question of whether the ending was integral to the text (see Velten 1930). Whether the ending was integral or not, questions still remain why such an addition was needed, what the reasons for its being added were, and what functions it had. Of course, the revision of the ending into a happy one was primarily done to adjust the text to the model of the fairy tale. A happy ending was considered indispensable for folktales. The imperative need for an ending seems to hold true in spite of Darnton's new research. In his controversial analysis of folktales, Darnton (1984) seems to suggest, in passing, that a "good ending" was not necessarily typical of all oral tales; "Little Red Riding Hood" served as a test case.

For at least two reasons this suggestion far from contradicts the view of "good ending" as a typical ending of the oral tale. Care must be exercised in using "Little Red Riding Hood" as an oral tale. Until published by Perrault, the text was not found as a written text. Indeed, it might well be that the French oral version, which was collected, of course, after Perrault had published *Les Contes*, stems from Perrault's written tale, of which the Brothers Grimm were well aware. If so (and most probably it is), then the fairy tale without a happy ending is simply the result of the transformation of the text from a written tale into an oral tale. In addition, it is worth noting that in a number of versions of "Little Red Riding Hood" presented by Delarue (1957), the good ending is indeed happy, as the girl does manage to escape. This seems to suggest that even before "crossing" the border, the teller of the tale could not tolerate the "bad ending" and felt it necessary to change it into a good one. The Brothers Grimm with their strong inclination to oral tradition, could not afford to violate this norm, as Perrault had deliberately done in order to signal his adult reader. Unlike Perrault, who officially addressed his tale to children, Brothers Grimm did not do so, at least not at first.

In fact, it was in the spirit of nineteenth-century Romanticism—a return to sources and nature—that the Brothers Grimm text was collected; accordingly, it addressed an adult audience. However, in spite of their longing for the real "roots," Brothers Grimm did not simply transcribe the tales. The romantic belief that Brothers Grimm had fanatically gathered folktales without at all changing them is no longer accepted today, although some scholars continue to cite the introduction to the first edition of *Kinder und Hausmärchen,* which says: "We have endeavoured to present these fairy tales as pure as possible . . . no circumstance has been added, embellished or changed" (preface to 1812 edition; Michaelis-Jena 1970, 53).

Most scholars agree that Brothers Grimm did change the original texts extensively. After the original handwritten manuscript of 1810 was found and compared to that published in 1812, major changes were discovered. Some scholars, like Rölleke (1975), even go as far as to describe the changes in terms of transformation into literary fairy tales and stylistically into Hochdeutsch in order to improve the literary quality of the texts. Others, like Zipes (1979b), describe the ideological transformation of the texts and their adjustment to their function in the socialization process. With regard to "Little Red Riding Hood" and other texts, Zipes claims that they are "decidedly biased against females who must either be put in their places or have their identity defined by males. The outcome is determined by the constraints of a conservative feudal ideology" (1979b, 136).

The Brothers Grimm could not and did not need to use Perrault's play between the "official" and "unofficial" reader. Like their nineteenth-century contemporaries, they believed that children, with their special needs, should be separated from adults. They also thought that these needs could not be supplied by the *Kinder und Hausmärchen,* at least not by the first edition; consequently, it had to be revised in order to become suitable for children. Brothers Grimm collected *Kinder und Hausmärchen* as evidence for the genuine and unspoiled material of the "Volksgeist." They did *not* do it in order to establish a body of children's literature. Their prime interest was a philological research, motivated by an ideology of a national return to the "roots." They wished to explore the "original" German language, and to restore to the German people the history of their language and its genuine vocabulary. Moreover, in referring explicitly to children's reading of *Kinder und Hausmärchen*, Jacob Grimm said that he never intended it for children, though it made him happy to find out that in fact they were reading it (letter to Arnim, 28 January 1813).

Because of the lack at this time of reading material produced solely for children, *Kinder und Hausmärchen* was read by children, which induced Brothers Grimm to adjust the text, especially from the stylistic point of view. It is also interesting to note that the great success of the first English edition of Grimm, published in 1823 and adapted for children by Edgar Taylor, encouraged Brothers Grimm to publish a collection of about fifty popular tales, modified for children in the same manner as the English edition. This edition, which unlike previous editions was illustrated, later became known as the *Kleine Ausgabe* and gained far greater commercial success than any of its predecessors.

The second edition of *Kinder und Hausmärchen* was therefore adjusted and changed, especially from the linguistic point of view. But even that was not enough, according to the Brothers Grimm. They felt that some parents might still find all or part of the book unsuitable for children, as they wrote in their introduction:

Dabei haben wir jeden für das Kinderalter nicht passenden Ausdruck in dieser neuen Auflage sorgfältig gelöscht. Sollte man dennoch einzuwenden haben, dass Eltern eins und das andere in Verlegenheit setze und ihnen anstössig vorkomme, so dass sie das Buch Kindern nicht geradezu in die Hände geben wollten, so mag für einzelne Fälle die Sorge begründet sein, und sie können dann leicht eine Auswahl treffen: im ganzen, das heisst für einen gesunden Zustand, ist sie gewiss unnötig. (Grimm, Reclam 1980, Band 1, 17)

[All the same, in this edition we haven't suggested satisfactory solutions for all problematic expressions concerning children. If parents claim that this item or other embarrasses them or disturbs them, so that they will be reluctant to leave the book in the hands of children, there might be cases where their worry is justified and they can easily choose: generally speaking, this is not necessary.]

In this passage appeared two new implied ideas that served as motivation for the changes which the text underwent during the century between Perrault and Grimm. The first was society's new perception of the child's distinct needs, and the second was the idea that those needs should be supplied under strict adult supervision. In fact, societal perceptions of childhood had changed in at least two senses: a new understanding of the nature of the child was evident, as well as a new demand that made adults responsible for the education of the child.

In Grimm's version of "Rotkäppchen," this new concept of childhood is expressed in the following three aspects: the relations in the family circle, the innocence of the child, and the need for instruction of the child. These aspects will be discussed in relation to different endings as well as in relation to other minor differences in the texts. As mentioned earlier, revision of the endings undoubtedly resulted from the need to adjust the text to the model of the fairy tale, requiring the Grimm's version to have a happy ending. However, this may not have been their only motivation and cannot serve as the only explanation.

It is quite possible that the source for the happy ending was, as Bolte and Polívka (1963) suggest, taken from "Der Wolf und die sieben jungen Geisslein" [The wolf and the seven young goats]; the "wolf" element was already part of the fairy-tale inventory and thus an almost ready-made solution. But, even if this claim is justified, it is still possible to account for the selection of this ending on the basis both of the model of the fairy tale and of the educational views at the time. Prevalent ideas about child education and the child as a potential reader (at least, since Grimm's second edition) demanded that the child learn a lesson from every event, experience, or story. Punishment and morality were an integral part of that learning process—Grimm's "Little Red Riding Hood" was no exception. It is interesting to note that the Brothers Grimm were happy with the ending from the educational point of view and even considered it as proof that the text was, indeed, suitable for children (see their foreword, Reclam 1980, Band 1, 17). Unlike the child in Perrault's version, the child of Grimm's version is given a chance to learn the lesson and apparently does so. The alternative endings might serve as an indication of the authors' hesitation between two endings. Yet they also fortify the educational message of the text. The Grimm's version shows that the girl, who promised at the end of the first conclusion that she would obey her mother, does keep her promise. When she next meets the wolf, she knows exactly what she is supposed to do—she does not stop to talk with him, but hurries to her grandmother, where both of them manage to trick the wolf. Thus the success of the lesson learned is proved. This sort of moral, unlike that of Perrault, did not address adults with an ironic wink of the eye. Moreover, unlike Perrault's moral that emphasizes the "gentleman," describing him in terms of the wolf, the Grimm's version does not emphasize the wolf-gentleman, but rather the child and the moral lesson that she must learn! These differences in emphasis are also the reason for the deletion of the erotic scene in the Grimm's version, which emphasizes the child's naiveté and innocence. As a result, the erotic characterization of the child was left out as was the erotic bed scene.

The Grimm's version does strongly emphasize a number of inter-family relations that are only hinted at in Perrault's version: the grandmother's love for the child, the mother's commitment to the grandmother, and the child's love for the grandmother. While the grandmother's love is hardly mentioned in Perrault's version, the Grimm's grandmother loves the child dearly; in fact, she sews the red hood as a symbol of her love. Thus, while the hood serves in Perrault's version to hint at the sexuality of the child, in the Grimm's version, it serves as a sign of the grandmother's profound affection for the child.

Cette bonne femme lui fit faire un petit chaperon rouge, qui lui seyait si bien, que partout on l'appelait le Petit chaperon rouge. (Perrault, Garnier 1967, 113)

[This good woman made for her a little red hood, which suited her so well that everyone called her Little Red Riding Hood.]

. . . am allerliebsten aber ihre Grossmutter, die wusste gar nicht, was sie alles dem Kinde geben sollte. Einmal schenkte sie ihm ein Käppchen von rotem Sammet, und weil ihm das so wohl stand und es nichts anders mehr tragen wollte, heiss es nur das Rotkäppchen. (Grimm, Reclam 1980, 156–57)

[. . . but most of all her grandmother, who did not know what else she could give to the child. One day she gave her as a present a little hood of red velvet, and as it became her so well and she did not want to wear anything else, she was always called Little Red Riding Hood.]

23

In Grimm's version the mother's attachment to the grandmother is stronger than in Perrault's version, where the mother sends the child because she herself is baking and because she fears that the grandmother is sick. In Grimm's version, the mother knows for sure that the grandmother is sick and sends the child to help her, showing that the mother feels responsible for the grandmother and family relations are much closer.

> Un jour sa mère, ayant cuit et fait des galettes, lui dit: "Va voir comme se porte ta mère-grand, car on m'a dit qu'elle était malade, porte-lui une galette et ce petit pot de beurre." (Perrault, Garnier 1967, 113)

> [One day her mother had fried and made the biscuits, told her: "Go and see how your grandmother feels, because someone told me that she was ill, take to her biscuits and this little pot of butter."]

> Eines Tages sprach seine Mutter zu ihm: "Komm, Rotkäppchen, da hast du ein Stück Kuchen und eine Flasche Wein, bring das der Grossmutter hinaus; sie ist krank und schwach und wird daran laben." (Grimm, Reclam 1980, 157)

> [One day her mother said to her: "Come, Little Red Riding Hood, here is a piece of cake and a bottle of wine, bring them to Grandmother; she is ill and weak and this will comfort her."]

Even relations between the child and grandmother seem to be less casual in the Grimm version. While the child gathers flowers for her own sake in Perrault's version, she does so in order to make grandmother happy in Grimm's version.

> . . . et la petite fille s'en alla par le chemin le plus long, s'amusant à cueillir des noisettes, à courir après des papillons, et à faire des bouquets des petites fleurs qu'elle rencontrait. (Perrault, Garnier 1967, 114)

> [. . . and the little girl went by the longer road, and enjoyed herself by picking hazelnuts, running after butterflies, and making bouquets of the little flowers she found on her way.]

> Rotkäppchen schlug die Augen auf, und als es sah, wie die Sonnenstrahlen durch die Bäume hin und her tanzten und alles voll schöner Blumen stand, dachte es: "Wenn ich der Grossmutter einen

frischen Strauss mitbringe, der wird ihr auch Freude machen."
(Grimm, Reclam 1980, 158)

[Little Red Riding Hood opened her eyes and when she saw how the
sunbeams dance here and there through the trees, and pretty flowers
grow everywhere, she thought: "If I bring grandmother a fresh nosegay,
this will also make her happy."]

Thus the different notions of the family in each period—the child-
centered family versus the loose family connections—found expression in the different presentations of the child and the family in
each of the texts. In addition, even more prominent differences can
be discerned between the two versions' ideas about education.

An educational system, in the modern sense of the notion, simply
did not exist in Perrault's time, nor did the need for systematic education of the child. In Grimm's time, however, education not only
existed, but was considered essential for the child's spiritual welfare.
Adults within and outside the family circle were considered responsible for the education of the child. This is best exhibited in Grimm's
version by the instructions given to the child by her mother. These
instructions—entirely missing from Perrault's version—express the
new ideas about education that had penetrated society in the hundred years between Perrault and Grimm. The mother instructs the
child to behave herself: "Und wenn du in ihre Stube kommst, so
vergiss nicht, guten Morgen zu sagen, and guck nicht erst in alle
Echen herum" [When you come into her room, don't forget to say
good morning and don't peep in every corner first.] (Grimm, Reclam
1980, 157). She also instructs the child not to leave the path:

"Mach dich auf, bevor es heiss wird, und wenn du hinauskommst, so
geh hübsch sittsam und lauf nicht vom Weg ab, sonnst fällst du und
zerbrichst das Glas, und die Grossmutter hat nichts." (Grimm, Reclam
1980, 157)

["Go now before it is too hot, and when you go, go nice and proper and
do not leave the path, otherwise you will fall and break the glass and
your grandmother will get nothing."]

The idea that children should be instructed by adults as far as their
behavior was concerned, a notion unknown in Perrault's time, was

commonly practiced in Grimm's time and served as a basis for the
relationship between mother and child in Grimm's text. Moreover,
the school, an institution that hardly existed in Perrault's time, had
become both established and hated. When the wolf meets the child,
he declares that she looks as sad as if she were going to school: "Du
gehst ja für dich hin, als wenn du zur Schule gingst, und ist so lustig
haussen in dem Wald" [You are walking along, as if you were going to
school, and it is so cheerful out here in the woods.] (Grimm, Reclam
1980, 157–58). The different ways in which childhood was perceived
also allowed different prospects for presenting the child. While the
naive country girl of Perrault is lost forever, the little girl of Grimm is
saved by adults who are responsible for her. As long as she is pro-
tected by them, she is safe, and that is exactly the moral she learns:
"Rotkäppchen aber dachte: 'Du willst dein Lebtag nicht wieder al-
lein vom Wege ab in den Wald laufen, wenn dir's die Mutter verboten
hat'" [But Little Red Riding Hood thought, "You will never again
leave the path if your mother has forbidden you to do so."] (Grimm,
Reclam 1980, 159). In the hundred years that passed between Perrault and Grimm, a new concept of childhood, the "instructive" concept, developed. This new concept differed from the previous one in
the importance it attached to the educational system and to books as
the main educational tools of such a system. In quite a short time, it
became the raison d'être of texts for children and guided their options and their norms; to a large extent, the new concept determined
what was appropriate and what was to be labeled as unsuitable. Thus
this concept was one of the main reasons for the changes that took
place in "Little Red Riding Hood" from Perrault to Grimm (needless
to say, along with many other important factors, including the literary
conventions and linguistic aspirations guiding the Brothers Grimm).
Moreover, it has governed, even more powerfully, writing for children since the time of the Brothers Grimm. This may be assumed
because the basic idea about writing for children, that is, that children's books should be written under the supervision of adults and
should contribute to the child's spiritual welfare, has not changed
since the middle of the eighteenth century (see chapters 6–7). What
has changed are the specific ideas prevalent in each period about
education and childhood. However, the idea that books for children
have to be suitable from the pedagogical point of view and should

contribute to the child's development has been, and still is, a dominant force in the production of children's books.

Nevertheless, changes in the specific ideas of education did result in a demand for the revision of certain elements in children's literature. For example, pedagogic views in England at the turn of the nineteenth century were responsible for the prohibition of fairy tales. As a result, the subject of fairies was excluded from canonized children's literature and found refuge only in underground literature (on the role of chapbooks in retaining fairy tales, see chapter 6). The educational establishment mistrusted works of imagination and favored the so-called "realistic" works, whose constant figures were death and sickness (for an exhaustive description of the texts, see Avery 1975, especially chapters 2–4). On the other hand, when the attitude toward imagination changed by the middle of the nineteenth century, or in Townsend's words, imagination was "rehabilitated," fairy tales were again introduced into the canonized children's system (for a brief description of this process, see chapter 6). Yet, because the mid to late nineteenth-century ideas about the child and his education were different from those dominant in Grimm's time, Grimm's "Rotkäppchen" was no longer considered appropriate and had to be revised in accordance with the new views.

Modern Adaptations of Grimm

The children's market of the Western world is practically flooded today with a considerable number of editions of "Little Red Riding Hood." The prolific production of the text is encouraged by its status as a "classic," which ensures its commercial success. It is also prompted by the great importance attached to the text on psychological grounds. Some psychologists even go so far as to declare that the text is indispensable for a child's development and that the child should be acquainted with the full version—no omissions at all are suggested (see Bettelheim 1976; for a serious criticism of him, see Zipes 1979c). Indeed, all modern editions of "Little Red Riding Hood" share (explicitly or implicitly) the same point of departure—the belief that the text should suit prevailing ideas about the child and childhood. Because of this belief, some editions changed the text only slightly or not at all in deference to the "complete version" approach of certain psychologists. Others—in fact, numerous editions—changed the text extensively. The basis for the textual revisions are assumptions held by the editors about childhood, especially about *the child's capacity to understand and the themes to which he should be exposed*. With these two issues in mind, the various adaptations are concerned mainly with the characterizations, the introduction of unsuitable events, and the assumed social norms of the texts and do not hesitate to change what is regarded as inappropriate for the child. The only difference between revisions lies in the solutions they offer for these problematic issues and the extent of deviation they exhibit from the original.

For a brief discussion of the handling of these aspects, three versions of "Little Red Riding Hood" were chosen randomly (almost any three versions will do; for analysis of other versions of "Little Red Riding Hood," see Nodelman 1978). These versions serve as a good example of the norms that determine the procedures of textual revision in accordance with the principles described above. The versions to be discussed here are the following: Modern Promotions, no date; Puppet Book, 1970; and A Pop-up Book, no date. All three agree about the need to revise the aspects of the tone, characterization, unsuitable events, and social norms in accordance with their understanding of the child and childhood.

THE TONE

The assumption that the child is the implied reader can be discerned by the tone of the text. In all versions, the tone is not only authoritative, but also superior and condescending. This becomes eminently clear when the narrator explains those points he presumes the child is incapable of understanding by himself. For instance, the narrator of the Puppet edition explains the name of the little girl in the following manner: "That is exactly why she was called Little Red Riding Hood." The same narrator also explains the craftiness of the wolf, assuming a child cannot comprehend such sophisticated behavior: "The crafty old wolf really knew where Grandmother lived. He also knew that the path across the meadow was the shortest way to

28

reach Grandmother's house." The narrator of the Pop-up edition is not sure a child can understand that the wolf disguised himself as the grandmother, thus he explains: "She was surprised to see her Granny in bed (You see, she thought the wolf was her Granny)."

ASSUMED SOCIAL NORMS

Very often the texts give expression to common social norms and prevailing fashions. This can be discerned not only in major structures, but in minor details as well. For instance, alcohol is a negative value and therefore will be replaced by fruit, honey, or milk in accordance with the modern "natural food" fad. Thus mother sends a varied basket to suit the current fashion: "One day her mother packed a basket with cake and fruit" (Puppet); or, "One day her mother told her to take a basket of bread and honey to her grandmother who was sick" (Modern Promotions). After the hunter rescues the child, grandmother makes a little party, and what does she serve but milk: "They were all so happy that they decided to have a party then and there. Grandmother served glasses of milk to her visitors" (Puppet). When it is the fashion to present the child with challenges he has to experience by himself, the text is revised into a "challenge" story; and the child is given a chance to experience a visit to her "granny" all by herself: " 'Oh yes, that would be lovely,' said the Red Riding Hood. 'I've never been to Granny's on my own before. It will be an exciting adventure!' So Little Red Riding Hood waved goodbye to her mother and started to walk along the forest path to Granny's cottage. As she walked along and saw all the birds and forest creatures she was not a bit frightened for she loved the forest" (Pop-up).

UNSUITABLE EVENTS

Any information that is considered unsuitable for children is either omitted or revised to make it acceptable. The text avoids both the violent scene where grandmother and child are devoured by the wolf and also any possible unpleasant information. This is probably the reason for the grandmother's not being "sick" in the Modern Promotions edition, but rather euphemistically "not well." Similarly in the Puppet Book, the mother explains, "This is a gift for you to take to your grandmother. She is not well and will enjoy eating some cake and fruit." In the Pop-up edition, nothing at all is wrong with grandmother: "Why don't you go and visit Granny? . . . I'm sure she would be pleased to see you." The various devices writers use to avoid the violent scene at the end are clear evidence of the attempt to avoid unsuitable information. The most extreme solution is to deny all violence and even prevent the wolf himself from being hurt: "When the wolf saw the hunter's long rifle, he had a change of mind. Now it was his turn to be frightened. He had time for just one yelp before running out of the house as quickly as he could" (Puppet). In other cases, the wolf does get punished and poetic justice is done. In most cases, however, the violent scenes with grandmother and the child are simply avoided. Grandmother hides in the closet without getting hurt, and the child is rescued *before* and not *after* the wolf devours her:

> But grandmother saw the wolf, too! She dashed into her clothes closet and locked the door behind her, doing it so quickly that the wolf hardly knew what was happening. (Puppet)

> At that moment a hunter passed the house. He heard Little Red Riding Hood's frightened scream and burst open the door. (Puppet)

> Fortunately, at that moment, the forester arrived. He ran inside and was just in time to rescue the little girl. Red Riding Hood breathed a sigh of relief when she realized what a narrow escape she had had. (Pop-up)

This examination of Perrault's, Grimm's, and three out of hundreds of modern versions of "Little Red Riding Hood" indicates that the changes in the texts were neither random nor insignificant. Many reasons lay behind these changes (for instance, prevailing literary models), but one of the crucial factors in determining the character of the texts for the child was undoubtedly the different concepts of childhood held by society. Since the eighteenth century, children's literature has been strongly linked with the educational establishment and has based its legitimation on it. This linkage has served as a source for constraints imposed upon children's literature in at least two areas: the way in which children are presented, characterized, and judged by the texts and the way in which the child is assumed to be the implied reader of the text.

Thus, children's libraries in the eighteenth, nineteenth, and twentieth centuries contain the same titles, but once the books are opened, it becomes quite clear that the contents vary considerably. What really counts is the way childhood is perceived by society, for it is society's perceptions that determine to a large extent what actually lies between the covers.

Texts

EDITIONS OF GRIMM

German Versions:
Rotkäppchen und andre Märchen von Gebrüder Grimm. 1947. Stuttgart: Herold Verlag.
Kinder und Hausmärchen gesammelt durch die Brüder Grimm. 1962. Munich: Verlag Heinrich Ellermann.
Rotkäppchen. 1965. Text nach Grimms Märchen. Zurich and Stuttgart: Rascher Verlag.
Die Schönsten Kindermärchen. Brüder Grimm. 1970. Munich: Verlag Heinrich Ellermann.
Janosch erzählt Grimm's Märchen. 1972. Weinheim and Basel: Beltz und Gelberg.
Rotkäppchen. 1972. Bad Aibling: Siebert Kinder Bücher.
Zauberwelt des Märchenwaldes. [1973]. Fürth/Bay: Pestalozzi Verlag.
Rotkäppchen. 1974. Zurich: Diogenes Kinder Klassiker.
Grimm Märchen. 1975. Munich: Annette Betz Verlag.
Grimm Märchen. Mein Erstes Buch. 1979. Edited by Richard Bamberger. Vienna and Munich: Jugend und Volk.
Zaubermärchen der Brüder Grimm. 1979. Bayreuth: Loewes Verlag.
Rotkäppchen; Schneewittchen. Mainz: Verlag Engelbert Dessart.

English Versions:
Red Fairy Book. (1890) 1950. Collected and edited by Andrew Lang. London, New York, and Toronto: Longmans, Green and Co.
Little Red Cap. 1965. Adapted by Evalyn Kinkead. New York: McGraw-Hill.
Little Red Riding Hood. Retold by Albert G. Miller. New York: Random House.

Little Red Riding Hood. 1968. London: Collins.
Little Red Riding Hood. 1970. (Puppet Story Book). Adapted by Oscar Weigle. New York: Grosset and Dunlap.
Red Riding Hood. Fairy Tale Pop Up Book. N.p.: Nutmeg Press.
Little Red Riding Hood. New York: Modern Promotions.

EDITIONS OF PERRAULT

French Versions:
Il était une fois, Vieux contes français. 1951. Paris: Flammarion.
Contes de Perrault. 1960. Paris: Editions Marcus.
Les contes de Perrault. 1976. Paris: Fernand Nathan.
Contes de ma mére L'Oye. 1977. Charles Perrault, Folio junior. Paris: Gallimard.
Les contes de Perrault. 1979. Paris: Marcinelle-Charleroi.

German Versions:
Märchen aus vergangener Zeit. 1965. Munich: Arena Meistererzählungen.
Märchen. [1967]. Vienna and Heidelberg: Verlag Carl Ueberreuter.

Chapter Two

The Self-Image
of Children's Literature

 In the previous discussion of the emergence of children's culture, I concluded that its status within culture as a whole and in the literary polysystem in particular is inferior. In a way this status is similar to that of non-canonized adult literature, mainly in some of its patterns of behavior such as its tendency to secondary models, to self-perpetuation, and so forth (see Even-Zohar 1979). A further similarity between the two systems can be seen in the fact that both are stratified not only by genre but also by subject and readership. The latter stratification manifests itself through a division by gender (men and women in adult literature; boys and girls in children's literature); and the former by a variance of subject matter—adventure, detective, school stories, and so on (see Toury 1974).

Yet, the position of the children's system should not be discussed, as is sometimes suggested, in terms of the non-canonized system. Such an identification is deceiving in that it belies the special status children's literature maintains in regard to the educational system and the literary system. It can also lead to a disregard for the distinction between non-canonized adult literature and the children's system, which by itself, is stratified as a whole into canonized and non-canonized systems. Another approach, which seems more helpful for my purposes of examining the status of children's literature in culture, is to focus on what might be described as its "self-image."

Social psychology has largely been concerned with the connection between social status and self-image—the way a certain group regards itself as a result of both internal and external points of view. It has shown that different social groups have different self-images

33

(Goffman 1959) which, to a large extent, determine their norms, motivations, and major patterns of behavior. This is why I have chosen to discuss the status of children's literature as it relates to the self-image of children's writers and to apply my conclusions metaphorically to the whole system of children's literature, whose poor self-image seems to result from the attitudes of various literary and social factors in culture.

The self-image of the children's system is determined, like any other self-image, by mutually dependent external and internal points of view of social factors in culture. The external point of view is associated with how other systems regard the children's system, while the internal is connected with the system's view of itself. These internal and external views are formulated in adjustment to one another and thus reinforce each other, in spite of the fact that they represent contradicting interests at times. The inability of a system to extricate itself from this "catch" is most evident when one tries to violate expectations resulting from those views. Even then one is forced to behave in accordance with them, or at least cannot avoid taking them into account.

Hence, a discussion of the self-image of children's literature can explore both society's expectations of the children's system, as well as the system's response to them. The discussion of self-image can serve as a good point of departure for studying characteristic patterns of behavior of the children's system, especially as far as norms of writing for children are concerned. The following two questions will be raised in discussion of these issues: How is self-image created and what are its main features? (How does the system see itself? How is the system seen by other systems?); In what way does self-image determine the character of the texts for children, or in other words, what sort of constraints are imposed on the texts for children as a result of its self-image?

Other Systems' Views of the Children's System

From the beginning, children's literature was regarded by other systems as inferior. The general attitude toward children's literature can be best exposed by viewing the means by which society attributed a high status to literary systems and their writers. These means, which have become status symbols, are beyond the reach of children's literature, as the following cases indicate.

Most children's books are not considered part of the cultural heritage, and hence national histories of literature barely mention children's books, if at all. Children's writers and books rarely appear as items in encyclopedias or lexicons, unless the latter are specifically devoted to children's literature. In such a way, a distinction is made between "real" literature and children's literature.

Children's literature has not been regarded as a subject of study at universities, because it was not considered a subject of importance in culture. Moreover, the recent change that took place in the attitude toward children's literature in curriculum only reinforces its inferior position; that is, although children's literature is taught in courses in many universities, it has not gained recognition as a subject for departments of literature (with a few exceptions). If anyone at all considers it as a legitimate field of research, then mostly departments of education do. Again, this is true because children's literature is not regarded as part of literature, but more as part of the educational apparatus—a vehicle for education, a major means of teaching and indoctrinating the child. In past centuries, adult literature was thought of in terms of its educational function in society, but here, this is not a case of adult literature's norms being perpetuated through the children's system, even though it may seem so. The linkage to the educational system is not the result of a transition of literary norms, but rather the result of social legitimations and motivations that have played an important role in the development of children's literature (see chapters 6–7) and since then have fixed the educational system as a major frame of reference for children's literature. A critical view of this linkage between children's literature and the educational system is sharply expressed by the writer Jill Paton Walsh: "Many teachers see the children's writer, like the children's doctor, the children's psychiatrist, the children's teacher, the children's home, as part of the apparatus of society for dealing with and helping children, as a sort of extracurricular psychiatric social worker" (Walsh 1973, 32).

Awarding prizes is one of the major means by which "people in culture" attribute high status to writers. So far, the policy of awarding prizes has almost always excluded children's writers from the list. Not even one Nobel Prize, nor any other less prestigious prize, has ever been awarded to a children's writer. In order to fight this blatant disregard for children's literature, special prizes for children's writers were established, as Lucia Binder observed: "When the International Board on Books for Young People under the initiative of its founder Jella Lepman decided to establish an international award for children's literature, it did so with the intention of creating a symbol of international cooperation, but also of finally giving the profession of writing for children the proper recognition which it had not hitherto received from the general public" (Binder 1977, 123). The establishment of special prizes for children's writers might have improved their position in society, but on the other hand, it also reinforced their lower status. What is actually implied by such a phenomenon is the belief that children's literature is something "different" that cannot be judged by "normal" literary criteria and thus needs special criteria of its own. A prominent example of the "non-literary" evaluation of children's literature is patently clear in the composition of juries awarding prizes to children's writers. These judges mostly come from the field of education (see, for instance, the *News* of the American Library Association and the description of the procedure for awarding prizes, Dohm 1957); what is even more telling, perhaps, are their reasons for making the award. Children's books deserving prizes are those which "deal with the real problems of children and which help them to understand themselves as well as other people and the world in which they live" (Binder 1978, 32). That is, it is the educational and not the literary value of the book which merits praise.

Thus, a writer for children is chosen to receive the most prestigious prize primarily because his work has such educational value. The jury decision for awarding the Hans Christian Andersen Medal to Paula Fox claimed:

> Children's books such as those by the American author Paula Fox, who was this year awarded the Hans Christian Andersen Medal, can help children *to develop understanding* for one another and also help the many adults who are having their own "Year of the Child" during the "Century of the Child" *to find a way of teaching the child and the adolescent.*

> In her movingly told stories Paula Fox has succeeded in capturing
> moments in the lives of children which *can be of decisive importance in
> their personal development.* (Binder 1978, 32; my italics)

The jury decisions reflect not only criteria for judging children's
books, but also society's expectations of children's literature, as Walter Scherf notes in an introduction to a list of prize winners: "Awards
reflect the views of an era. The lists of prize-winning titles give evidence of our period's ideas on education more forcefully and authen-
tically than it could be found anywhere else" (Scherf 1969, vii). As
most protocols reveal, the jury expresses the view that a children's
writer should respond to the child's needs, a demand which some
writers find hard to accept, as Jill Paton Walsh states: "A teacher once
asked me why I didn't write a book about trade unions, for surely I
would agree there was a need for one. Another teacher . . . asked
'But don't you feel any responsibility to your audience?' Now this is
like being asked 'have you stopped beating your wife?' It contains an
accusation" (Walsh 1973, 30).

This poor self-image of a children's writer is most evident when
compared to the self-image of the canonized writer for adults. Writers for adults serve not only as the frame of reference of the literary
establishment but also enjoy the status of "serious" members of society. Their views on societal issues are warmly welcomed and even
encouraged, while a writer for children is seldom asked for his view
and rarely finds himself considered part of the literary establishment.
This social position forces him to constantly protect his status in
society, which consequently remains peripheral and apologetic.

The demand to respond to the child's needs, however, is neither
simple nor unequivocal. The children's writer is perhaps the only
one who is asked to address one particular audience and at the same
time to appeal to another. Society expects the children's writer to be
appreciated by both adults (and especially by "the people in culture")
and children. Yet this demand is both complex and even contradictory by nature because of the different and even incompatible tastes of
children and adults. But one thing is clear: in order for a children's
book to be accepted by adults, it is not enough for it to be accepted by
children. "Good literature is *good* literature; it satisfies both children
and critics," claims the critic Rebecca Lukens (1978, 452–53).

This assumption about children's literature is oversimplified and even untrue most of the time. The criteria for a positive evaluation of a children's book, if it is not an educational one, is its success in appealing to adults. As José Miguel de Azaaola, president of the prestigious Hans Christian Andersen Award confessed when awarding the prize to Meindert DeJong, "I do this because his books have deeply moved me, because their impressions will not soon be forgotten by me" (International Youth Library, Hektograph no. 697, p. 3). Whether or not the book "deeply moved" a child seems not to be taken into account at all. This, strangely enough, happens in spite of the increasing awareness of adults of the differences between themselves and children—a distinction that adults are keenly aware of and even endeavor to make sharper. Nevertheless, when it comes to evaluating children's culture, they ignore the child's opinion and focus on the adult's.

In such a way, external attitudes toward children's literature both contribute to its poor self-image and concurrently create it. Children's literature is thus deprived of all status symbols. At the same time, it must cope with contradictory criteria imposed on it by the need to satisfy both adults and children and by the need to respond to what society believes to be "good" and appropriate for the child. The fact that children's literature is not recognized as literature per se and the criteria for its evaluation are not determined by its official addressee influences, of course, the view children's writers have of themselves. Consequently, it plays an important role in determining the self-image of the system from the internal point of view.

The Internal Point of View

Historically speaking, the status of the writer for children has always been inferior to that of the writer for adults, which probably explains the following two phenomena.

For quite a long time (long after adult writers had ceased the practice, see Charvat 1968a), writers for children (especially men) would not sign their work. Most likely, they were interested in writing for children because of the chances for commercial success or because of ideological motivations. Nevertheless, they tended to publish anonymously or under a pseudonym, probably because writing for children was not respected by society, as Peter and Iona Opie noted when describing their work on their anthology:

> At the beginning of the nineteenth century moralists and educators customarily had their names on the title pages of their work; but those who sought to entertain the public remained discreet about it. They were not held to be advancing man's spiritual and intellectual welfare like their calf-bound contemporaries, and could not therefore expect to be admired. In only one of the frolics we chose, for instance, was the full name given of its author. (Opie and Opie 1980)

With women, however, the case was different. Having a subordinate position in society, women writers had nothing to lose. On the contrary, by writing they could only improve their status, especially because writing for children was considered more appropriate for women, who were "closer" to children. As a result, most of the official writers for children during the eighteenth century and the beginning of the nineteenth century were women.

Today, however, this is no longer true: children's writers do sign their works. Men and women in equal numbers write for children and are equally respected. Yet, most writers seem to be unhappy with their position in society as children's writers. It could be almost a rule that when highly praised and unquestionably recognized writers for children are asked about being such, they are usually reluctant to "admit" it. The following extracts may serve as evidence for writers' feelings about being children's writers and the profession of writing for children.

> Not long ago, I spoke at a girls' boarding school where I was asked over and over again, "Why do you write for children?" My immediate response was, "I don't." Of course I don't. I don't suppose most children's writers do. (Madeleine L'Engle, in Townsend 1971, 127)

> I have never written for any age-group at all, but merely for myself.
> . . . The themes of my children's books are mostly quite adult, and in fact the difference between writing for children and for adults is, to me at any rate, only a quite small gear change. (Rosemary Sutcliff, in Townsend 1971, 201)

Books of mine which are classified officially as books for children were not written *for* children. (Scott O'Dell, in Townsend 1971, 160)

Is there a conscious difference in the way I write for grown ups and children? No, there is no difference of approach, style, vocabulary or standard. I could pick out passages from any of the books and you would not be able to tell what age it was aimed at. (L. M. Boston, in Townsend 1971, 36)

Each book I have written I have desperately wanted to write. Whether or not they had anything to do with children has never occurred to me. I have never liked children's books very much, I don't read very many. (Jane Gardam 1978, 489)

Patricia Wrightson "admits" that she writes for children but describes her writing for children as a stage toward her writing for adults: "So I ventured to try my hand at a novel for children, very deliberately making my work into a course of training; requiring that in each book I should break new and (for me) difficult ground, and hoping to graduate to adult novels some day" (Townsend 1971, 212). How can we account for this phenomenon? What is the explanation for the fact that well-known writers for children who attained their status as children's writers are reluctant to view themselves as such? In fact, the only writer to admit openly that there is a difference in writing for children and for adults is someone well known as an adult writer like Bashevis-Singer (1977), who, when interviewed on the issue of writing for children, confirmed: "If I have to torture someone, I would rather torture an adult than a child" (1977, 12). Pamela Travers, Maurice Sendak, and Jill Paton Walsh seem to hint at the roots of the problem. Pamela Travers explains why she rejects the title of a children's writer in the following manner: "Nor have they [my books] anything to do with that other label: 'Literature for children,' which suggests that this is something different from literature in general, something that pens off both child and author from the main stream of writing" (1975, 21). Jill Paton Walsh makes these insightful observations: "Very often the decision that they are children's writers was made in the first instance by a publisher. Once made it is difficult to alter. . . . We live in an age of shrinking literacy and it seems we must accept that books which give us pleasure to write and our own adult friends pleasure to read, will appeal in the world outside only to the unsophisticated and the young" (1973, 32). Maurice Sendak adds: "We who work on children's books inhabit a sort of literary *shtetl*. When I won a prize for *Wild Things*, my father spoke for a great many critics when he asked whether I would now be allowed to work on 'real' books" (Kanfer 1980, 41). What is common to all these writers is the feeling that writing for children means something inferior, something different from "literature" as understood by highbrows. They feel that as writers for children they are doomed to an inferior status as writers and are unduly restricted in their writing because of society's attitude toward children's literature. Thus, because of the poor self-image of children's literature, writers attempt to liberate themselves from the children's system and wish to be considered simply as writers (or potential writers) for adults in order to better their position and to gain more freedom in their writing. This wish is manifested first in the writer's denial of a particular addressee (the child) and the denial of any distinction between writing for adults and writing for children. As a result, children's writers claim that children's and adult literature deserve the same respect. The second manifestation of the desire to be "liberated" lies in the assertion that children's books should be judged by the same criteria as adults', or in C. S. Lewis's words: "I am almost inclined to set it up as a canon that a children's story which is enjoyed only by children is a bad children's story" ([1952] 1969, 210). These claims of children's writers indicate the pervasiveness of the poor self-image of children's literature. Not only does the outside world regard children's literature as inferior, but also the children's writers themselves do so, thus reinforcing and perpetuating this self-image. However, despite the explicit denial of the special status of children's literature, it cannot be denied that writers for children do write within the framework of constraints imposed on the system due to the specific addressee. But this specific addressee turns out to be problematical, because of the contradictory necessity of appealing to both adults and children at the same time. Writers find various solutions to this problem, the most extreme being the ignoring of one of the addressees. Either the child is used as an excuse only (see the case of ambivalent texts in chapter 3) or the adult reader is ignored, which entails risking his rejection. The first case is described by Astrid Lindgren as follows: "Many who write for children wink slyly over the heads of their

41

child-readers to an imaginary reader; they wink agreeingly to the adults and ignore the child" (1978, 12). The opposite extreme is characteristic of writers of popular literature, who are mainly interested in the commercial success of their books and do not expect any prestigious standing in society. They are concerned not with whether their books will be able to appeal to adults, but with whether they will sell well. This is why they are ready to pay almost any price, including a total rejection by adults, in order to enlarge their reading public and increase the popularity of their books. This readiness is evident not only in the fact that they totally ignore adults as potential readers, but more so in their presentation of adults in the texts. Typical in these texts is the creation of a world where a strong opposition between children and adults is presented—a world in which children can do anything without adult help and even manage to do it better. Adults seldom take part in their adventures, and if they do, they are either fought against or mocked at, or both (for an analysis of such a case, see chapter 4 on Enid Blyton). Yet these two ways for challenging constraints imposed on children's literature are rather extraordinary. Most writers for children do not endeavor to bypass these constraints, but accept them as a framework for handling the problem of their specific addressee. The need to take the addressee into consideration is primarily evident in the assumptions the writer maintains about the possible understanding of the text by its reader—the child—or, in other words, the writer's assumptions about the possible realization of the text by its implied reader. Following Hrushovski (1979) and Vodička (1976), I do not refer here to a specific realization of the text by an individual reader, but to the construction of the reading process, which is the intersubjective result of the realization of the text as assumed by the writer, consciously or unconsciously.

Writers are well aware of the potential realization of the text by its implied reader, especially in regard to the following aspects (which, of course, are mutually dependent): the text's complexity, the structure of the narration, the stylistic level, and the subject matter. The last two seem to bother writers most because they are the aspects that, in their eyes, make children's literature distinct or, in the words of Nina Bawden: "But you can, and should, leave out things that are beyond their comprehension" (1974, 9). Or, as Astrid Lindgren observes: "First of all, the language. I think this is almost the most important thing . . . if you are writing for five-year-olds . . . then you shouldn't use words and expressions which you must be at least 10 years old to understand. . . .

Write things which are funny for children and adults; but never write something which you know for sure is funny only for adults" (1978, 10–11). Writers are also well aware of the structure of narration and the text's complexity. Nina Bawden referred to the structure and nature of narration in the following manner: "The only real difference between writing for adults or for children is whose eyes I am looking through" (1974, 13). Moreover, Gillian Avery, when being interviewed by Naomi Bowen, explained why her book addressed children, in relation to complexity: "I realised it couldn't possibly be an adult book, everything is far too simplified, all the emotions are far too direct for it to be considered as an adult book" (Bowen 1975, 207).

A Test Case: Roald Dahl's *Danny the Champion of the World*

THE TEXT AND THE IMPLIED READER

Writers' descriptions of their work and their attitudes toward it can serve as a very good source for analyzing their self-image, but cannot serve as the ultimate evidence for manifestations of the self-image on the text. Once the question of the text arises, the texts themselves must be studied to inquire into their specific addressee. The structure of the specific addressee is, of course, best revealed when compared to that of the adult as implied reader. One can see the virtue of comparative analysis of texts transferred from the adult to the children's system (*Gulliver's Travels* and *Robinson Crusoe*, for instance), where the systematic constraints of the implied reader are responsible to a large extend for the transfer procedure (see Chapter 5 on translations for children). But comparison as such demands the elimination of other issues involved with the translation procedure before the question of the implied reader can be discussed (especially when a text is not only "translated" from adult to children's system, but also from one national literary system to another). Hence the best possible example for illustrating the point is a text that was written by the same writer for children and then for adults and exists at the same time within the literary polysystem.

This text, despite being a rare phenomenon, can serve as a good example to reveal the writer's constraints (regarding the child as an implied reader) because all the methodological eliminations required for such a comparative study preceded the text processing. In such a case, it is undoubtedly the writer's recognition of different implied readers that is responsible for the text's differences, and not the differences between two literary polysystems and their norms or different poetics of different writers. The trouble is, of course, the rarity of such cases. First of all, not many writers write for both children and adults. Secondly, if they do, as a result of being aware of the differences between the two readers, they write very different "stories."

Such a unique case does exist in Roald Dahl's "The Champion of the World," a story originally written for adults and published in his book *Kiss Kiss* (Dahl [1959] 1980). Later, Dahl rewrote the story as a novel for children entitled *Danny the Champion of the World* (Dahl [1975] 1977). Another good reason for choosing this text as a test case lies in its nonconventionality. In terms of the children's system, the text is not a standard text at all. Both its subject (poaching) and the relations described between father ("thief") and son are exceptional (In a private conversation with Mrs. Kay Webb, a former editor of Puffin Books, I was told that she questioned whether the book should be published at all, due to its "inappropriate" subject). Yet, this is exactly why Dahl's texts are interesting; when the non-conventional children's text is compared to the adult text, fundamental differences, which are undoubtedly the result of different implied readers, are revealed.

It is true that at first glance the two texts might seem very similar: both tell the story of fantastic poaching of pheasants and fantastic tricks that make the hero the champion of the world in poaching. Moreover, both are narrated in the first person. When analyzed, however, the two texts turn out to be quite distinct because one is much more complicated than the other. By saying that a text for adults is more complicated than one for children, I refer both to the organization of the various levels of the text, as well as to the interlevel relations. Hence in the text for adults, various levels are not organized according to the simplest (or most immediate) principle.

For instance, the distribution of material is not chronological but is organized by the narrator's consciousness. On the other hand, the interlevel relations of the adult text are aimed at carrying more functions by fewer elements (for instance, the relations between the order of information and the narrator carry both the function of irony, the characterization of main characters, evaluation of poaching, and more).

The most obvious differences between the adult and children's versions are in the following aspects: genre (short story versus novel); characters and characterization (two friends versus father and son); attitudes (ambiguous attitudes versus unequivocal attitudes); and endings ("open" ending versus "happy" ending). These differences cannot be simply explained as the result of differences between the main characters, nor can they be accounted for simply as a difference between a short story and a novel. Both decisions concerning genre and characters (and consequently, attitudes and endings) were directly related to Dahl's original decision to "translate" the adult short story into a text for children. As a famous writer, Dahl could afford to write on "inappropriate" subjects and describe unusual relations between father and son. If he still wished to ensure the acceptance of the text by the children's system, however, he had to offer compensation for violating the rules by adapting both subject and characters to the children's code. Therefore, a certain change in direction was not a matter of free will but was imposed on the text due to its transfer to the children's system.

The most obvious step Dahl had to take was to "neutralize" the subject by legitimizing both the subject and the attitudes presented in the text. To do so, he had to enlarge the text to permit a different presentation. Therefore the first decision—that of a generic change—was made because of the need to have much more scope than the ambiguous and undetermined attitudes the adult short story required. Of course, the decision to turn it into a novel might have had commercial ground as well—novels sell better. But even if this were not the case, Dahl would still have had to make it into a novel if he desired to integrate different attitudes into the text. This point can be best illustrated by analyzing the narrator and the structure of the narration, the attitudes toward poaching, and the endings of each of the texts.

THE NARRATOR AND THE STRUCTURE OF NARRATION

Despite the fact that the two texts are narrated in the first person (and thus can be described as formally having the same point of view), they are totally different in the nature of the narrator, in his tone and attitude toward the story related, and in the distribution of material and order of information.

In both texts, almost the same information is related. Yet, the distribution of the information and its interpretation vary, aiming to achieve a different characterization of the narrator and to determine different value judgments. Hence, in the children's version, the narration is motivated by a realistic model, whereas in the adult version, the motivation is the narrator's own consciousness. Of course, both texts are reconstructions of events that happened to the narrator, or in Perry's words: "The narrating 'I' transmits the information to the reader 'now,' while following the sequence in which it had 'once' come to his knowledge as the experiencing 'I'" (1981, 38). Still, the adult version tries to mask the reconstruction (as opposed to the children's version, which emphasizes it) because it contributes to the retrospective judgment of the narrator. The narrator of the children's version tries to reconstruct his understanding as a child—not in order to question it—but rather to reinforce and justify it. In spite of the many years that have passed, he still identifies with the child's attitude toward his father. He still admires him and hardly criticizes him at all:

> Because what I am trying to tell you . . .
> What I have been trying so hard to tell you all along is simply that my father, without the slightest doubt, was the most marvelous and exciting father any boy ever had. (*Danny the Champion,* 173)

The adult version, in attempting to mask the reconstruction, emphasizes the limited consciousness of the narrator by creating the impression that the information is given in the very same order it occurred, without judging it in retrospect. This is done by opening "in medias res," by motivating the order of information purely on the narrator's consciousness and by emphasizing the narrator's lack of information. Thus, the story opens just before the two friends are about to leave for their night adventure: "All day, in between serving customers, we had been crouching over the table in the office of the filling station, preparing the raisins" (*Kiss Kiss*, 206). From this point on, the night's events unfold, as seen through the eyes of one of the two friends—Gordon. The children's version, on the other hand, opens in the earliest possible point of time, mainly in order to create an all-knowing narrator: "When I was four months old, my mother died suddenly and my father was left to look after me all by himself" (*Danny the Champion*, 7). The narrator of the children's version possesses all the information and the ability to understand and evaluate not only the story told, but also the behavior of the world. He is not only authoritative, but patronizing as well. When he is not sure his reader can follow him, he bothers to explain what life is all about, as indicated in the following examples:

So watch out, I say, when someone smiles at you with his mouth but his eyes stay the same. It's sure to be a phony. (*Danny the Champion*, 13)

Most of the really exciting things we do in our lives scare us to death. They wouldn't be exciting if they didn't. (*Danny the Champion*, 51)

In the adult version, however, the narrator sometimes lacks the information and sometimes even the ability to comprehend it. Frequently, the text emphasizes his lack of information by leaving events unexplained, at least until the narrator comes to understand them. For instance, Gordon knows that Claud comes back empty-handed and that the next day there will be something like pheasant to eat. Only very late does he understand the connection between the two (poaching pheasants and fooling the keepers), and only later is this mystery solved in the text: "He seldom came back until very late, and never, absolutely never, did he bring any of the spoils with him personally on his return. But the following afternoon—and I couldn't imagine how he did it—there would always be a pheasant or a hare or a brace of partridges hanging up in the shed behind the filling station for us to eat" (*Kiss Kiss*, 208–9).

The authoritative narrator of the children's version never reveals such ignorance. He never leaves events unexplained only to have them explained later. Almost everything is explained, and usually in unequivocal terms. Moreover, the narrator always puts himself in position to rightfully judge whatever is told. This characterization of the narrator might have contradicted the other effect the text creates, that of reconstructing the child's point of view. In quite a few places, the text stresses the narrator's understanding as a child. For instance, when Danny first finds out about poaching, the text reconstructs his astonishment at the time: "I was shocked. My own father a thief! This gentle, lovely man! I couldn't believe he would go creeping into the woods at night to pinch valuable birds belonging to somebody else" (*Danny the Champion,* 30). Another example is his fear when he does not find his father at home:

> I looked in the office. I went around and searched behind the office and behind the workshop.
> I ran down the field to the lavatory. It was empty.
> "Dad!" I shouted into the darkness. "Dad! Where are you?" . . .
> I stood in the dark caravan and for the first time in my life I felt a touch of panic. (*Danny the Champion,* 27–28)

However, this potential contradiction is not used by the text for creating complex attitudes because the adult narrator practically accepts all of the child's view. The whole idea of introducing two points of view was not aimed at creating clashes; on the contrary, it was brought up for the sake of reinforcing and justifying the narrator's attitude toward his father. In the whole text there is not even a single phrase where the distance in time is used to illuminate a different view that he held as a child, nor even to contradict an earlier view. The distance in time between the narrator and the narrated story only emphasizes the fact that time has not changed his attitude toward whatever happened. Only when it is compared to the adult version does the function of the distance in time become clear. In the latter, it is of a different nature: the narrator does not identify with the story told, and the clash of attitudes between Gordon and Claud creates the ironical tone of the text.

Hence, what constitutes the basis for any literary work—the reconstruction of events—is used by both adult and children's versions to achieve different evaluations of the narration and consequently different tones. This is best reflected in an examination of the handling of the main issue, poaching, in both texts.

ATTITUDES TOWARD POACHING

In the adult version the two friends do not share the same attitude toward poaching. While Claud is very enthusiastic about poaching and regards it as a prime symbol of wit and cleverness, Gordon is, at best, indifferent. Thus, for instance, Claud is very proud of his methods of poaching, while Gordon does not hesitate to remark that he suspects their originality and effectiveness (remarks which Claud ignores either because he is too dumb to understand or because he deliberately wishes to avoid them):

> "You pay out the line about fifty yards and you lie there on your stomach in the bushes waiting till you get a bite. Then you haul him in."
> "I don't think your father invented that one."
> "It's very popular with fishermen," he said, choosing not to hear me.
> "What is Method Number Three?" I asked.
> "Ah," he said. "Number Three's a real beauty. It was the last one my dad ever invented before he passed away."
> "His final great work?"
> "Exactly, Gordon." (*Kiss Kiss*, 212)

The clashes between the two friends—Gordon understands ironically, or he is, at least, very skeptical of that which Claud takes seriously—contributes to the ironical tone of the text (which is also the result of the distance between the narrator and the narrated story). Such an ambiguous attitude is inconceivable in terms of the children's system, which assumes that children cannot comprehend such complex relations and therefore require unequivocal ones. Hence, in the children's version, Danny and his father share a single attitude—both are excited and enthusiastic. When they leave for poaching, his father asks:

> "How do you feel, Danny?"
> "Terrific," I said. And I meant it. For although the snakes were still wiggling in my stomach, I wouldn't have swapped places with the King of Arabia at that moment.

Moreover, Danny remarks on his father as follows: "I could see my father becoming more and more twitchy as the excitement began to build up in him" (*Danny the Champion*, 111–12). The need to determine unequivocal attitudes on the one hand and to set father on the "good side," to present him in positive terms on the other, leads to a long series of legitimations of poaching in the children's version. While the adult version encourages ambiguous values and evaluates poaching ambiguously, the children's version presents it unequivocally in black and white. The opposition between good and bad (particularly in the evaluation of poaching), deliberately blurred in the adult version, becomes delineated in the children's version.

In the adult version, poaching moves along on an axis that has two poles—from crime to sport. At first the information presented by the narrator creates the impression that the two friends, Gordon and Claud, are about to do something sinister, very close to crime. But nothing is really determined yet. If the reader builds the hints scattered in the text into a definite structure, he might as well have expected a gun. But, surprisingly enough these hints end up dissolving in the relatively harmless sequence of "poaching with the help of raisins." However, this quite harmless structure appears in the text as a better organizing structure only after the "criminal" option is built into the text:

> "What's under there?" I asked.
> . . . "To carry the *stuff*," he said *darkly*.
> "I see."
> "Let's go," he said.
> "I still think we ought to take the car."
> "It's too *risky. They'll* see it parked."
> "But it's three miles up the wood."
> "Yes," he said. "And I suppose you realize we can get *six months in the clink if they catch us.*" (*Kiss Kiss*, 207, my italics)

By the time the reader eventually finds out that it is nothing really criminal and that the story refers to poaching only, the sense of something criminal has already been built into the text, and despite its negation, it still attributes a negative value to poaching.

In the children's version, the very device of constructing options to be cancelled later is impossible, because the text, by its very nature, cannot permit multifaceted opinions. Yet, it should be noted that the option to consider poaching in terms of a crime is not avoided; on the contrary, it is presented in the text mainly in order to reject it and to give way to the other ultimate option, namely, the legitimation of poaching. At first the text does not avoid the possibility that poaching constitutes stealing, and Danny is even shocked by the discovery about his father:

> "You mean *stealing* them?" I said, aghast.
> "We don't look at it that way," my father said. "Poaching is an art."
> (*Danny the Champion*, 30)

However, quite soon after, Danny accepts his father's view in the same way he accepts anything else: "Yes, I believe you" (*Danny the Champion*, 32). This acceptance becomes possible thanks to the buildup of Danny's father, as well as to the order of the narration.

The story does not begin with the mysterious preparations for poaching as does the adult version; rather, the first chapters give a very positive buildup of the father. He is portrayed as an honest man, universally liked and adored by his son as the best possible father, even when his son examines him in retrospect:

> During my early years, I never had a moment's unhappiness or illness.
> (*Danny the Champion*, 8)
> My father without the slightest doubt was the most marvelous and ex-
> citing father any boy ever had. (12)
> He was a marvelous story teller. (13)
> My father was a fine mechanic. People who lived miles away used to
> bring their cars to him for repair rather than take them to the nearest
> garage. (17)
> It was impossible to be bored in my father's company. (19)
> So you can see that being eight years old and living with my father was a
> lot of fun! (25)

Only after the best possible buildup of the father is fabricated does the narrator bring up the subject of poaching as his father's "deep dark secret." But the option to regard it as "dark" and criminal is almost immediately rejected, because such a wonderful father could not possibly be involved in something dark or criminal. From this point on, until the end of the story, poaching is justified in various ways. Hence, once the alternative of viewing poaching as stealing is rejected, the other option is accepted; this, of course, stands in contrast to the adult version in which an ambiguous evaluation of poaching, either as a game or as stealing, is maintained continuously and simultaneously.

How is the legitimation of poaching achieved? Undoubtedly, Dahl's decision to legitimize poaching meant that he had to strive for a sound justification of poaching in order to alter its normal reputation, which usually is very close to crime. This can perhaps explain why he chose to justify poaching on the basis of at least three alternative and mutually reinforcing value systems. Poaching is presented in the children's version both as a local game that has its own code of conduct as well as an act of social justice. And, if that is not enough, it is also motivated by the legitimate desire for revenge by the father. Dahl's efforts to justify poaching in all possible ways is made clear when compared to the attitudes toward poaching in the adult version. Here, poaching has almost no justification and is presented as a sort of obsession: "He was more purposeful about it now, more tight-lipped and intense than before, and I had the impression that this was not so much a game any longer as a crusade, a sort of private war that Claud was waging single-handed against an invisible and hated enemy" (*Kiss Kiss*, 209). Its possible social justification is only hinted at, but this option (as with any other option in the adult version) is not developed. For example, Claud remarks in one passage: "I had heard it said that the cost of rearing and keeping each pheasant up to the time when it was ready to be shot was well over five pounds (which is approximately the price of two hundred loaves of bread)" (*Kiss Kiss*, 216). The possibility of regarding poaching as a local game is limited to Claud's point of view and is not reinforced by anyone else. In fact, Claud does claim that everybody is involved with poaching, thus encouraging the idea of poaching as a game. Nevertheless, even his best friend, Gordon, is involved only for the first time, and the only one proven to have been involved was Claud's good-for-nothing father, a fact that only reinforces Gordon's skeptical view, who remarks:

"I thought you said your dad was a drunk."
"Maybe he was. But he was also a great poacher, Gordon. Possibly the greatest there's ever been in the history of England. My dad studied poaching like a scientist."

"Is that so?"
"I mean it. I really mean it." (*Kiss Kiss*, 210–11)

In the children's version, all three justifications—social justice, revenge, and local game, which were only hinted at in the adult version—become definite and terminal. The element of social justice
appears in the following sequence: when explaining to Danny what
poaching is all about, his father claims that historically poaching was
the way hungry people managed to feed their families and hence was
socially justified. Poaching is thus represented as part of a conflict
between social classes: " 'Let me tell you about this phony pheasant-
shooting business,' he said. 'First of all, it is practiced only by the
rich. Only the very rich can afford to rear pheasants just for the fun of
shooting them down when they grow up. These wealthy idiots spend
huge sums of money every year buying baby pheasants from pheasant
farms and rearing them in pens until they are big enough to be put
out into the woods" (*Danny the Champion*, 32–33). Poaching also represents the only honorable way for poor people to feed their families:

> Mind you, in those days, just about every man in our village was out in
> the woods at night poaching pheasants. And they did it not only be-
> cause they loved the sport but because they needed food for their fami-
> lies. When I was a boy, times were bad for a lot of people in England.
> There was very little work to be had anywhere, and some families were
> literally starving. Yet a few miles away in the rich man's wood, thou-
> sands of pheasants were being fed like kings twice a day. (*Danny the
> Champion*, 30–31)

The element of revenge also surfaces in the children's text. But
unlike the obsessive Claud of the adult version whose crusade is not
really justified by the text, both father and son are enthusiastic (but
not obsessively so) and seem to have good reason for their crusade.
Danny's father declares war on Mr. Hazel (spelled Hazel in the adult
text and Hazell in the children's) only after Mr. Hazel breaks the
code of the game and humiliates Danny's father by making him fall
into the pit, which was "the kind of trap hunters in Africa dig to catch
wild animals" (*Danny the Champion*, 61). After the father manages to
escape from the pit, Mr. Hazel continues to humiliate him daily:

"You know what makes me so hopping mad," he said to me all of a sudden. "I get up in the mornings feeling pretty good. Then around nine o'clock every single day of the week, that huge silver Rolls-Royce comes swishing past the filling station and I see the great big bloated face of Mr. Victor Hazell behind the wheel. I always see it. I can't help it. And as he passes by, he always turns his head in my direction and looks at me. But it's the *way* he looks at me that is so infuriating. There is a sneer under his nose and a smug little smirk around his mouth, and although I only see him for three seconds, it makes me madder than mackerel." (*Danny the Champion*, 78–79)

The desire for revenge is strengthened both by the negative characterization of Mr. Hazel and by other people's disgust at Hazel's attempt to break the rules of the game. Thus, it is not only Danny's father who regards Mr. Hazel's pit as wrong; indeed, it is the respected doctor who describes it as "diabolical": "It's worse than that, William! It's diabolical! Do you know what this means? It means that decent folk like you and me can't even go out and have a little fun at night without risking a broken leg or arm" (*Danny the Champion*, 72). Even if Mr. Hazel had not broken the traditional rules of the game, he would have deserved revenge. The black-and-white characterization of the text leaves no doubt as to where he belongs. It is true that, in both texts, Mr. Hazel is characterized as snobbish and the worst kind of "nouveau riche." But, the source for this description in the adult version is the limited consciousness of the narrator, while the children's version deliberately reinforces the narrator's view of Mr. Hazel by other respectable views, such as the doctor's. There is no doubt that Mr. Hazel is nasty to everybody, boys and dogs included:

"No," my father said, "I do not like Mr. Victor Hazell one little bit. I haven't forgotten the way he spoke to you last year when he came in for a fill-up."
I hadn't forgotten it either. . . . "Fill her up and look sharp about it. . . . And keep your filthy little hands to yourself. . . ."
". . . If you make any dirty fingermarks on my paintwork," he said, "I'll step right out of this car and give you a good hiding." (*Danny the Champion*, 42)

Moreover, Mr. Hazel was also nasty to the doctor's dog: "I saw him get out, and I also saw my old dog Bertie dozing on the doorstep. And do you know what this loathsome Victor Hazell did? Instead of stepping over old Bertie, he actually kicked him out of the way with his riding boot" (*Danny the Champion*, 72–73). Apparently, he did not hesitate to cause troubles and make life difficult for Danny and his father: "There was little doubt, my father said, that the long and powerful arm of Mr. Hazell was reaching out behind the scenes and trying to run us off our land" (*Danny the Champion*, 44).

Furthermore, Mr. Hazel did not hesitate to break the traditional game, which had risks, rewards, and rigid rules known to all the village people (whose view the text ultimately adopts). Unlike the adult version, in the children's version practically everybody participates in poaching and therefore approves of it. Dahl is careful to pick up representatives of different classes so that no one (except for the "nouveau riche" Hazel) escapes poaching, not the doctor, not the vicar's wife, nor even the school headmaster. The following passage reveals the wide spread of "culpability," even of respected figures:

> "Dad," I said, "What on earth are you going to do with all these pheasants?"
> "Share them out among our friends," my father said. "There's a dozen of them for Charlie [the driver] here to start with. . . ."
> "Then there'll be a dozen for Doc Spencer. And another dozen for Enoch Samways——"
> "You don't mean *Sergeant* Samways?" I gasped. . . .
> Sergeant Enoch Samways, as I knew very well, was the village policeman. (*Danny the Champion*, 138)

Hence, even the respected representative of the law—Sergeant Samways—is involved. To Danny's even greater astonishment, the vicar's wife also participates in the village activity:

> "Mrs. Clipstone delivers everyone's pheasants," my father said. "Haven't I told you that?"
> "No, Dad, you haven't," I said, aghast. I was now more stunned than ever. (*Danny the Champion*, 139)

In fact, he ultimately spurns the possibility that poaching be regarded as a crime. Moreover, Mrs. Clipstone's involvement almost makes it into a social must. Again, what has been only hinted at in the adult version—the option of regarding poaching as a local game with its own code—becomes in the children's version definite and terminal.

Attitudes toward poaching are at the core of both texts, though in each they are used for different purposes. In the adult version, they illustrate the relationship between two friends—one stupid and obsessive, and the other one (from whose point of view the narration takes place) smart and ironical. In the children's version, attitudes toward poaching are used to expose unusual relations between father and son. However, the children's version strives to legitimize whatever the father does and endeavors to leave no open questions— hence, the multiple motivations and justifications of poaching in the children's version. This opposition between a text with strongly justified motivations and a text without such is best illustrated when the two endings are compared.

THE TWO ENDINGS

At first glance, the ending of the children's version might look unconventional—it is not the traditional "good ending" of a children's story. Perhaps Bashevis-Singer's words best reflect that traditional approach: "I try to give a happy ending to a story for a child because I know how sensitive a child is. If you tell a child that a murderer or a thief was never punished or never caught, the child feels that there is no justice in the world altogether" (1977, 12–13). In the children's version, Dahl's ending appears to break with conventional endings as the father's beneficent plans are not fully accomplished. Thus, a whole year's supply of pheasants is lost as Danny's and his father's methods fail—the sleeping pills dissolve and Mrs. Clipstone's poor baby is beaten terribly by the awakening pheasants, a scene which is both comic and frightening at the same time.

Danny's father is also mocked for the first time at the story's end, his "ingenious" idea to carry the pheasants during the daytime through the village turns out to be a catastrophe:

> "There's only one way of delivering pheasants safely," he said, "and that's under a baby. . . ."
> "Fantastic!" the doctor said. . . .
> "It's brilliant," Doc Spencer said. "Only a brilliant mind could think of a thing like that." . . .

"There's more than one hundred pheasants under that little nipper," my father said happily. (*Danny the Champion,* 147)

"He'll be having a very comfortable ride today, young Christopher," my father said. (148)

"She seems in an awful hurry, Dad," I said. "She's sort of half running." . . .
"Perhaps she doesn't want to be caught in the rain," he said. "I'll bet that's exactly what it is." . . .
"She could put the hood up," I said.
He didn't answer this. . . .
My father stood very still, staring at her. . . .
"What's up, Dad?"
He didn't reply. (149)

My father let out a cry of horror. . . .
"Great Scott!" Doc Spencer said. I know what's happened!
It's the sleeping pills! They're wearing off!"
My father didn't say a word. (151)

"They nearly pecked him to pieces!" she was crying, clasping the screaming baby to her bosom. (153)

While the ending might appear unconventional in terms of the children's system, when compared to the adult version, it is clear that Dahl deliberately tried to transform it into a "good" ending. The constraints of the implied reader in the children's version are particularly evident as opposed to the open endings of the adult version. In the former, the narrator pulls together all the threads; poetic justice is done, no issue remains open. In the adult version, however, the story opens and ends "in medias res." It ends when the two friends, with a bitter sense of failure, close the filling station and leave the place, only hinting that Mr. Hazel's shooting party was ruined. But except for that subtle suggestion, they get nothing. They do not have a chance to see that their revenge was successful, nor do they even get any pheasants to eat. In contrast stands the children's version, in which the shooting party was ruined with "all those fancy folk . . . driving in from miles around in their big shiny cars and there won't be a blinking bird anywhere for them to shoot" (*Danny the Champion,* 138). In addition, Mr. Hazel is publicly mocked and his precious car is damaged. The justice of revenge is thus fully accomplished:

They were all over the roof and the bonnet, sliding and slithering and trying to keep a grip on that beautifully polished surface. I could hear their sharp claws scraping into the paintwork as they struggled to hang on, and already they were depositing their dirty droppings all over the roof. . . .

In less than a minute, the Rolls was literally festooned with pheasants, all scratching and scrabbling and making their disgusting runny messes over the shiny silver paint. What is more, I saw at least a dozen of them fly right *inside* the car through the open door by the driver's seat. Whether or not Sergeant Samways had cunningly steered them in there himself, I didn't know. (*Danny the Champion*, 160–61)

It also seems that Dahl did not wish to leave the beloved characters with the slightest sense of failure, only to laugh at them a little. Hence, unlike the adult version, where the ingenious device totally fails and all the pheasants fly away, in the children's version, Dahl finds a way to leave some pheasants for a good feast. The dear doctor manages to find a way to hide some and everybody gets his share: " 'Two for you, Grace, to keep the vicar in a good mood,' Doc Spencer said. 'Two for Enoch for all the fine work he did this morning. And two for William and Danny, who deserve them most of all.' " (*Danny the Champion*, 167). Moreover, Dahl ends the adult version with an ominous phrase:

"You go on home, Bessie," Claud said, white in the face.
"Lock up," I said. "Put out the sign. We've gone for the day." (*Kiss Kiss*, 233)

But the narrator of the children's version concludes the story as follows: "What I have been trying so hard to tell you all along is simply that my father, without the slightest doubt, was the most marvelous and exciting father any boy ever had" (*Danny the Champion*, 173).

The differences described above between the two versions result from Dahl's preliminary assumptions about different implied readers in each of the texts. These assumptions led to the most fundamental differentiation between the two—the generic. The decision to adapt the short story into a novel was imposed on the text because of the need to present poaching in the children's version as a well-justified and properly motivated activity. This decision resulted in both central and peripheral structural differences between the adult and the children's versions, which were all rooted in the assumptions about a different potential realization of the text. This difference in potential realization encouraged each text to differentiate in the following aspects: the narrator (limited and ironical versus authoritative and identifying); and the structure of narration (different distribution of material resulting in different structuring of the texts; complex process of filling gaps versus a simple one). The need to change the value judgment of the adult version was another outcome of Dahl's assumptions about potential realization. Dahl could not afford to leave the ambiguous values and characterizations present in the adult version; such a presentation would be inconceivable in terms of the children's system, as children are supposed to understand only unequivocal attitudes. Hence, the text for children offers a clear opposition between "bad" and "good," and the characterization is of a black-and-white nature.

The analysis of Dahl's texts was presented in order to illustrate how assumptions about the formal addressee impose constraints on a text, even when the text is not conventional within the children's system. No doubt these constraints, so powerful and demanding, are the prime reasons for the reluctance of writers to admit to being children's writers and thus contribute, in large measure, to the reinforcement of the poor self-image of the children's system.

Texts

Dahl, Roald. [1959] 1980. "The Champion of the World." In *Kiss Kiss*. London: Penguin, 206–33.
———. [1975] 1977. *Danny the Champion of the World*. Harmondsworth, Middlesex: Puffin Book.

Part Two

SOLUTIONS

Chapter Three

The Ambivalent Status of Texts

 As discussed earlier, the poor self-image of the children's system imposes various inflexible constraints on the text,[1] such as the simultaneous (often contradictory) need to appeal to both the child and to the adult and the tendency to self-perpetuation, the acceptance of only the well known and extant and the reluctance of the system to admit new models.[2] Although most writers for children do indeed write within the framework of these constraints, some try to overcome them through two extreme solutions: rejecting adults altogether (typical of the non-canonized system; see chapter 4); and appealing primarily to adults, using the child as an excuse rather than as a real addressee (typical of the canonized system). These solutions, which produce ambivalent texts, will be analyzed and discussed in this chapter, by exploring characteristic features of ambivalent texts (typical structures, uses of prevalent norms, manipulations of implied reader) and then by examining the need to produce ambivalent texts on the basis of the systemic constraints of the children's system.

The Notion of Ambivalence

Once a text is produced (written, published, and distributed) at a certain point in time, it occupies a particular position in the literary

---

[1] Writing in the frame of constraints is not typical only of children's literature, as any written text is to some degree a result of constraints of a certain model. In other systems, however, more flexibility is permissible.

[2] The willingness of an inferior system to accept the well-established models alone is characteristic not only of other systems in the literary polysystem, but also of other semiotic systems, especially of social systems (see Even-Zohar 1978b).

polysystem, determined by the different constraints of the literary polysystem and the literary life (see Even-Zohar 1978b, Shavit [1978] 1982). The text acquires then a certain status that later may change in accordance with the dynamic changes of the literary system. But at a given point, in a given period, a text normally has an unequivocal status in the system it has entered. This status can be described in terms of binary opposition: either the text is for children or for adults, either it is canonized or non-canonized.

Most literary texts maintain an unequivocal status; some texts, however, maintain a status that cannot be described as unequivocal but rather as diffuse. The phenemenon of a diffuse status, well known in other semiotic systems, such as social systems, implies that a certain sign (in this case a literary text) enters into more than one opposition of status within the same system. Those texts that have a diffuse status could not be dealt with as long as a static notion of literature prevailed in literary theory; this static notion prompted the tendency to classify texts into well-defined, homogeneous, and closed categories, since the notion of structure was wrongly identified with the notion of homogeneity.

Today the dynamic concept of literary systems is quite accepted, and it is understood that the literary system is not static but is "a multiple system, a system of various systems which intersect with each other and partly overlap, using concurrently different options, yet functioning as one structured whole, whose members are interdependent" (Even-Zohar 1979, 290). This understanding enables scholars to describe the relations between systems and elements in terms of open categories: thus, theoretically it becomes possible to assume that diffuse boundaries and statuses exist—an assumption that was previously inconceivable with the notion of closed categories. Moreover, this understanding of the nature of literary systems need not necessarily assume that a system is homogeneous; rather it is possible to assume that a system is composed of heterogeneous and even contradictory elements and models (Even-Zohar 1979). For this discussion, the theoretical possibility of studying diffuse status and contradictory functions cannot be exaggerated, because the status of the texts in question is by definition not unequivocal but diffuse. That is, we are dealing here with a group of texts that normally belong to the children's system, although their being read by adults is a sine qua non for their success.

Scholars find it difficult to study and account for texts read by adults that at the same time are considered classics in children's literature—that is, texts which formally belong to one system (the children's) and still are read by the reading public of another system (the adult), yet their system attribution is based on the criterion of audience age (children versus adults). Moreover, these texts, officially and originally labeled as children's literature and occupying a dominant position at the center of the canonized system for children, often have to be rewritten (abridged and simplified) in order to become comprehensible and fully realized by children.

In this chapter I describe the ambivalent status of this group of texts and discuss their adaptations into books for children by the original writer himself as well as by various translators. The point of departure of the discussion is the dynamic notion of the literary system as developed by the pioneers of semiotics in Russia (Tynjanov 1971, Jakobson, 1960, 1971) and their followers (Even-Zohar 1979, Lotman 1976a, 1976b). Lotman's notion of ambivalence (1977) is of special importance for this discussion, although it needs reformulation to suit the analysis of this specific group.

In Lotman's discussion of the system's ability to change and renew itself, he points out the opposition between univalent and ambivalent texts. He describes the latter as those texts that give the system "its flexibility and the heightened degree of non-predictability in its behaviour. It is for this reason that the internal capacity of the object for creating information (the inexhaustibility of hidden possibilities) is far greater than its description would indicate" (1977, 201). Unfortunately, Lotman's notion of ambivalence is too broad, for it encompasses at least three different kinds of texts: texts which have survived many literary periods, functioned differently in each, and consequently were read differently during each period (for instance, the drastically different interpretations of *Oedipus Rex* during its more than two thousand years of existence); texts which, from the historical point of view, changed their status in the literary polysystem, that is, were pushed from periphery to center and vice versa, from adult to children's literature (for example, the transfer of Dickens's novels to the children's system after losing their status in the adult system); and texts which should or can be realized simultaneously in two different ways by the same reader at the same time in order to be fully realized (for instance, Henry James's *The Turn of the Screw;* see

Hrushovski 1974, Perry and Sternberg 1968). Thus, Lotman's notion of ambivalence refers to a vast range of different texts. According to his concept, almost any text could be described, from the historical point of view, as ambivalent, because almost every text has historically changed its status in the literary polysystem due to the dynamic nature of that system.

Unlike Lotman, I propose a reduction of the scope and the range of the notion of ambivalence in order to apply it to one specific case only: texts that synchronically (yet dynamically, not statically) maintain an ambivalent status in the literary polysystem. These texts belong simultaneously to more than one system and consequently are read differently (though concurrently), by at least two groups of readers. Those groups of readers diverge in their expectations, as well as in their norms and habits of reading. Hence their realization of the same text will be greatly different (see Ben-Porat 1978).

The notion of ambivalence, as described above, is most helpful in studying well-known texts of children's literature such as *Alice in Wonderland, Watership Down, Winnie-the-Pooh, The Little Prince,* and *The Hobbit,* of whose peculiar status many have been aware, though the reasons for this status have scarcely been discussed. In describing this group of texts, which became in society's eyes *the* texts of children's literature, it is necessary to both characterize their features as well as account for their tendency to continually maintain a diffuse status. Toward these purposes, this chapter will focus on the writer, the reader, and the structure of the text by discussing the following questions: What does a writer achieve by producing an ambivalent text? What is the structure of the ambivalent text and how does it function in each system? How is the text realized differently at the same time by two different groups of readers (in this case, children and adults)? In other words, how does the structure enable the text to address two different audiences?

The Writer

Writing for children usually means that the writer is limited in his options of text manipulation if he wants to assure acceptance of the text by the children's system. An ambivalent text provides the writer for children with a larger range of options in manipulating the text than does an univalent text. The writer has the otherwise inconceivable option of producing a text composed of models that are in disagreement with the children's system. As a matter of fact, the text's models are also in disagreement with the prevalent models of the adult system (otherwise they could have been accepted as texts for adults); it is exactly their disagreement with each of the systems, and the fact that they could not be exclusively accepted by either, that makes possible their simultaneous acceptance by both systems.

Historically speaking, ambivalent texts tend to manipulate models that are already rejected by the adult system but are not yet accepted by the children's. However, once the ambivalent text is admitted, thanks to the adult approval, into the center of the children's system, the way opens for the new model to be accepted. In this manner, the text becomes subject to imitations and is usually described as constituting a historical turning point. Yet the acceptance of the new model into the system does not necessarily mean that the texts following it will be as sophisticated as the original ambivalent text. Quite the opposite is true. Once the new model is accepted, the following texts need not be as sophisticated, and more often than not they will be based on a much more simplified and reduced version of the original model that they try to imitate. At the time of publication, however, the text must be rejected by one system or the other in order to be accepted by each. Only by addressing the text both to children and to adults and by pretending it is for children can the writer make possible the dual acceptance of the text. Adults are willing to accept it as a text for children because they are able to read it, due to its level of "sophistication" ("sophisticated" for the children of course). Their "stamp of approval" on the other hand, apparently opens the way for acceptance of the text by the children's system (though children do not realize the text in full and are not even supposed to do so, according to adult criteria). In such a way, the writer for children is not only able to overcome many of his limitations in writing for children, but is also able to ensure acceptance of the text that otherwise would have been rejected by both systems.

By having two groups of readers, the writer not only enlarges his reading public and reaches those who otherwise would not have read the text (because it was "merely" a children's book), but also ensures the elite's recognition of the dominant status of the text in the canonized children's system. The writer can therefore reinforce his status in the literary system and ensure a high status for his text in the children's system. Moreover, the ambivalent text often manages to occupy immediately a position at the center of the canonized children's system, in spite of the fact that univalent texts based on new models are usually rejected by the center of the system and are forced to fight their way from the periphery toward the center in a long and agonizing trail. Rarely do they manage to accomplish this goal.

Accordingly, the ambivalent status permits the writer, from the system's point of view, to produce a text composed of new models, thus breaking the prevailing norms that occupy the center of the system. In such a way, the writer is able to change existing norms in the children's system without risking his status and the status of the text. As a matter of fact, the writer of the ambivalent text can use the text as a key to his success and recognition.

The Structure of the Text and Its Function in Each System

What makes possible the appeal of the ambivalent text to two groups of readers from the structural point of view is the fact that the text is composed of at least two different coexisting models—one, more established, and the other, less so. The former is more conventional and addresses the child reader; the other, addressing the adult reader, is less established, more sophisticated, and sometimes based on the distortion and/or adaptation and renewal of the more established model. This is accomplished in several ways: by parodying some elements; by introducing new elements into the model (sometimes from another established model); by changing the motivation for existing elements; by changing the functions and hierarchy of elements; or by changing the principles of the text's segmentation.

The occurrence of coexisting models in a single text is known from other cases, such as parody. However, unlike parody, where one of the models is used to parody another (see Ben-Porat 1979), the manipulation of the two models in the ambivalent text is different, at least in some respects. Despite its inevitable parodization, the more established model is meant to be fully and simply realized by the child reader *as it is*. It is only the adult reader who is meant to realize the two coexisting models. What makes this double reading possible is the mutual exclusivity of the models structuring the text; it is as if one of the models, the more conventional, permits full realization without taking the other model into account, simply because the other model excludes it. In fact, the child reader is indeed supposed to ignore the less conventional model, while the interplay of the two models, the more and the less established, can be realized by adults only.

The dual structuring of the text also enables it to function differently within each system at the same time. Since it is ambivalent, the text may be accepted more easily by the center of the canonized system of children's literature, despite its new models. Hence the text can challenge the reluctance of the center of the canonized system (or any formal center in other semiotic systems) to admit new models as it endeavors to preserve the well established. The ambivalent text is then able to bring into the system new models (which might have existed, as such, only on the periphery of the system) and participates in the mechanism of change in the literary norms. Historically speaking, texts of this kind, once accepted, become models for imitation and are thus considered as opening a new period in the history of this literature. From the historical point of view, this diffuse status explains why a greater number of ambivalent texts tend to be produced during transitional periods and why there are fewer in stable periods.

However, while the ambivalent text functions importantly in the process of change of norms in the center of the canonized system for children, it is no more than "accepted" by adults as a "good" children's book. The text is accepted by adults only because it fulfills their requirements in regard to children's literature. All the same, this acceptance is crucial to the text as it determines and reinforces the status of the text in the children's system. Due to its dual structuring, the text manages to break the prevailing norms and at the same time to achieve a prominent status within the center of the system, whose norms the text violates. The text attains very high recognition in the children's system despite the fact that it is incompletely realized by children and that children prefer the adapted and abridged versions. This claim, however, does not mean that children are indeed incapable of realizing the full version. Unfortunately, almost any reliable information is lacking on how children do indeed realize texts and in what way it is different from that of adults. Most of the available information is too speculative and has no sound scientific basis. What is known for sure is that children are supposed to be able to realize texts differently and are brought up on different norms of realization; because of this, they are supplied with simplified texts that are supposed to respond to their abilities. This state of affairs makes the following phenomenon possible in the literary polysystem: the existence of a text that maintains a high status in one system (the children's) but is still simultaneously, and often primarily, read by the reading public of the other system (the adult).

The Reader

It is, as previously claimed, the dual structuring of the text that enables it to address deliberately two different groups of readers: adults and children. The opposition between the two groups is not only of age group (or in other cases of social class); what really matters is the differences in reading habits and in norms of textual realization of the two groups of readers. Each group will realize the text differently because each is accustomed to different norms of realization; opposition between them can be described as the opposition of norms of greater structuring and norms of lesser structuring of the text.

The writer, who always assumes the existence of a certain implied reader in producing his text, assumes in the case of the ambivalent text two different implied readers. The first is composed of adults who belong to the elite consumers of the canonized system for adults where (since the Romantic period) the norm of complexity and sophistication is prevalent. These consumers demand a high degree of complexity from the text and would realize such a complicated text in full. It was never intended that the other assumed implied reader, the child, would understand such a text, because society presumes his inability to do so. Thus, for this reader, who is accustomed to reduced and simplified models, the text offers the well-recognized established models and assumes that this less sophisticated reader will ignore certain levels of the text.

An institutionalized indication of the opposition among assumed readers (in their preferences for a more or less sophisticated version) is manifested in the existence of both annotated and abridged versions (see Gardner 1977, Disney 1980). The annotated version not only indicates the high status of the text but a certain level of sophistication that legitimates annotations. As Gardner claims in his introduction to the *Annotated Alice:* "It is only because adults—scientists and mathematicians in particular—continue to relish the *Alice* books that they are assured of immortality. It is only to such adults that the notes of this volume are addressed" (1977, 8). Hence, the annotated version addresses highbrow adults, while the abridged texts, which tend to be based upon the well-established model only, are addressed to children.

In such a way, unlike other texts that assume a single implied reader and a single (though flexible) ideal realization of the text, the ambivalent text has two implied readers: a pseudo addressee and a real one. The child, the official reader of the text, is not meant to realize it fully and is much more an excuse for the text rather than its genuine addressee.

A Test Case: *Alice's Adventures in Wonderland*

Several well-known texts for children can be described as ambivalent; some, like *The Hobbit* and *Winnie-the-Pooh*, are perhaps among the most famous texts for children. However, *Alice's Adventures in Wonderland* has been chosen for discussion mainly because it was Lewis Carroll himself who wrote three different versions of the same story, attributing a different status to each. The existence of Carroll's three different versions of *Alice* makes it more convenient, from the methodological point of view, to explore the nature of the ambivalent text because the differences between the three versions indicate the characteristics of the ambivalent text. The discussion of the differences between the three versions is further motivated by the fact that in principle the three versions differ from one another in the same way as adaptations of *Alice* for children, produced by several writers, differ from *Alice's Adventure's in Wonderland* (see, for instance, Disney 1980, Octopus 1980, and Modern Promotions, n.d.).

71

Carroll's three versions differ from one another primarily in the status attributed to them by the writer; only one of them was meant to be an ambivalent text, while the other two maintain an univalent status. When Carroll decided to publish *Alice* (see below), he decided to change the first version, probably because he found that version too sophisticated to be accepted by the children's system, yet not sophisticated enough to be accepted by adults. This is why most of the features characteristic of the ambivalent text already appear in the first version. But there is a crucial difference between the first and the second versions: various features, which are only hinted at in the first, become the dominant features of the second. Thus, the difference between the two versions lies not only in the presence or absence of certain elements, but in their organization and consequently their hierarchy within the text as well. In working on the second version, Carroll was clear in his direction; he wanted to expand those elements that can be described by us as giving the text its ambivalent nature. On the other hand, when writing the succeeding version, *The Nursery Alice*, Carroll eliminated and deleted all those elements that he had elaborated in the second version. In this third version, Carroll tried to extricate the text from its ambivalent status and deliberately transformed it in order to appeal solely to children, thus making it a univalent text.

In this discussion, the contrast between the two manipulations of the text, that of the ambivalent text and that of the univalent, will be studied to detect and uncover by such comparison the features of an ambivalent text. As in the comparison of an original versus a translated text, the comparison of the different versions, based on different models, enables us to recognize and expose the more conventional and the less conventional features of each of the models. Thus, Carroll's three versions make it possible to describe the text processing (Wienold 1981) and account for it, and to demonstrate different options for manipulating existing models within the system to which the text was attributed.

It is worth noting that translators, who adapted the text for children, acted, in principle, precisely as Carroll did, without being acquainted with the simplified version, *The Nursery Alice*. That is to say, they deleted systematically all the elements which together created the sophisticated model and based their adaptations on the more established model only.

THE THREE VERSIONS OF *ALICE'S ADVENTURES IN WONDERLAND*

Carroll wrote three different versions of *Alice's Adventures in Wonderland*. The first one, entitled *Alice's Adventures Underground*, was
given to Alice Liddell, the daughter of Dean Liddell of Christ
Church, on 26 November 1864 as a Christmas present. This version
was not published as a book for almost twenty years, and only in
March 1885, after Carroll's second version became very successful,
was the manuscript published. As the fascimile edition indicates, the
first version was primarily published as a historical document, and
not as a book for children, probably because Carroll wanted a more
ambivalent text. The well-known text, that of *Alice's Adventures in
Wonderland*, was the second version, written by Carroll after his
friends encouraged him to publish as a book the manuscript they had
had the opportunity to read. It is said that the novelist Charles
Kingsley found the manuscript in Liddell's house and urged Mrs.
Liddell to persuade the author to publish it. But Carroll was not
convinced until George MacDonald read it to his children with overwhelming success (Green 1960, 35). Still, Carroll was dissatisfied
with the fact that it was not "ambivalent enough." As a result, he was
reluctant to publish the first version as it was and changed much of it.
This version became the best known, and, in quite a short time,
became a children's classic, making Carroll very famous. Within two
years thirteen thousand copies were sold, although Carroll (who had
to pay for most of the publishing expenses) did not expect it to sell
more than five or six thousand.[3] Green claims that: "The two books
had become accepted classics with old and young well before the end
of the century and could be quoted without reference or excuse in

[3] Neither Carroll nor his publisher hoped for a commercial success. Carroll persuaded MacMillan to accept the book on a commission basis. Carroll was to pay for
the illustrating, printing, and engraving (see Wood 1966, 74), and after he decided to
withdraw the first edition, he described his commercial perspective in his diary of 2
August in the following manner: "Finally decided on the re-print of 'Alice' and that
the first 2,000 shall be sold as waste-paper. . . . If I make £500 by sale this will be a
loss of £100 and the loss on the first 2,000 will probably be £100 leaving me £200 out
of the pocket. But if a second 2,000 could be sold it would cost £300 and bring in
£500, thus squaring my accounts; and any further sale would be a gain; but *that I can
hardly hope for*" (Green 1949, 63, my italics). However, Carroll was surprised that
" 'Alice,' far from being a monetary failure, was bringing him a very considerable
income every year," as his biographer and nephew Stuart Dodgson Collingwood
claims (1898, 104).

the sure knowledge that all readers would take the allusions on the instant" (1969b, 57).

Queen Victoria's enthusiasm for the book, which became a legend in itself, only reinforced its status, and the fact that it was sold at the very high price of seven shillings and sixpence made it into a commercial success as well.[4] This commercial success became possible because the book was bought by adults for their own reading; normally, people were reluctant to pay so much for a children's book. Carroll himself was aware of the fact that his book was quite expensive and was not happy about it at all. On 15 February 1869, he wrote to Macmillan, his publisher: "My feeling is that the present price puts the book out of the reach of many thousands of children of the middle class" (Hudson 1978, 129).

In discussing the three versions of *Alice*, two questions will be raised: From the historical point of view, what did Carroll try to achieve by producing an ambivalent text? On what model is the structure of the text based and how does this structure enable the text to address two different audiences?

HISTORICAL BACKGROUND

When Carroll wrote *Alice*, the norms of the Romantic movement with its enthusiasm for the fantastic and fairy tales not only reigned in English literature, but practically governed the center of adult literature. In fact, by the 1860s, the Romantic movement had already begun to wane. The decline of Romanticism in the canonized adult system and the rise of the norms of Realism did not imply a sudden vanishing of the norms of the Romantic movement. Rather, as is often the case, the declining norms were pushed to the periphery of the literary polysystem—to the children's system. Hence the chil-

---

[4] Carroll's success was not immediate and could not be taken for granted. He did his best to make the book known to the elite and hoped they would approve of it, as Wood claims: "Dodgson sent out seventy presentation copies of *Alice* and he made sure that many of these went to well-known writers and artists and to others whose opinions and influence would spread the fame and increase the sale of the little red book" (1966, 75). However, not all reviewers were enthusiastic about the book, as the *Atheneum*'s comments show: "Mr. Carroll has laboured hard . . . and we acknowledge the hard labour. . . . We fancy that any real child might be more puzzled than enchanted by this stiff, overwrought story." (Cripps 1983, 38).

dren's system served, as in many other historical examples, as a perpetuating agent. It absorbed norms that had lost power in the adult system, but which began to function as the new norms of the children's system. This process is not surprising and does not need to be discussed in terms of "gesunkenes Kulturgut." Rather, it can be seen as a normal result of the relations between the adult and the children's systems.

In this case, the acceptance of the norms of Romanticism into the children's system became possible, from the literary system point of view, only when the norms of Romanticism began to decline in the adult system. This was true because the conservative children's system is usually ready to accept new norms only after they have been widely accepted in the culture. But usually by the time cultural norms are widely accepted, they have already begun losing their power as dominant norms in the center of the adult system.

The Romantic movement's passion for fantasy enabled the admittance of the genre into children's literature as well, though the process of the introduction of the fantasy model into the system was not easy, nor immediate. As expected, fairy tales and fantasy were not accepted into the children's system until they were first accepted by the adult system. This process itself became possible through translations of French, German, and Danish texts into English (that of Perrault, Grimm, and Andersen respectively). Thus the introduction of the new model into English children's literature was achieved through cultural interference (see Even-Zohar 1978c), and only after the new model had been accepted and legitimized by the adult literary system.

Hence, Carroll was not the first to write a fantasy story. On the contrary, he was preceded by several texts that opened the way for *Alice's Adventures in Wonderland* and made its acceptance possible. The text was nevertheless conceived of as a turning point in the history of English children's literature. For example, some histories do not even hesitate to divide the entire history of children's literature into "before *Alice*" and "after *Alice*" (see Muir 1969). But if Carroll *was not* the first to introduce the model, how did the text gain such historical status? The answer seems to lie both in the understanding of the process of the model's introduction into the children's system, as well as in Carroll's manipulation of the model.

At the beginning of the nineteenth century, the prevailing norms in the center of canonized English children's literature continued to be didactic and realistic. Thus the publication of a selection of fairy tales in 1809 that was revised by Benjamin Tabart (see Avery 1971) was, for the canonized system, rather exceptional, although the book did have a very strong moral tendency. Fairy tales were forbidden by the educational establishment and were widespread only in the non-canonized literature read by children in the form of chapbooks (see chapter 6). Consequently, with the exception of the French fairy tales, which were translated into English prior to the Romantic movement (1699, translation of Madame d'Aulnoy's *Contes des Fées*, published in 1721–28 in three volumes; 1729, Perrault's *Histoires du temps passé*), fairy tales were quite rare in English children's literature. For example, in September 1831, an anonymous critic, writing in *The Ladies Museum*, did not hesitate to bid good riddance to fairies: "The days of *Jack the Giant Killer, Little Red Riding Hood*, and such trashy productions are gone by, and the infant mind is now nourished by more able and efficient food" (Avery 1971, 321). Fairy tales began to be widespread in children's literature only toward the middle of the nineteenth century, when there was a flood of fairy-tale translation, both oral and written, which determined the dominance of the fantasy model in children's literature. To mention a few examples: Grimm was translated into English in 1823–26, and Andersen in 1846 (both by Mary Howitt); in 1854, a translation of a German collection, *The Old Story-Teller* by Ludwig Bechstein, was published; and in 1857 Annie Keary's translation of *Heroes of Asgard* was issued. In the next two years two more collections were published: *Four and Twenty [French] Fairy Tales* in 1858 and *Popular Tales from the Norse* in 1859. The "invasion" of fairy tales into English children's literature is evidenced by no less than four volumes of Andersen published in 1864: *Wonderful Stories for Children* from the Danish by Mary Howitt (Chapman and Hall), *Danish Fairy-Legends and Tales* (no translator is given, but it probably was Caroline Peachey), and *A Danish Story Book* and *The Nightingale and Other Tales*, both translated by Charles Boner from German versions (Hürlimann 1967, 51).

However, translations turned out to be just the first in the overflowing stream of original fairy tales and fantasy stories to be published in the following years. Among the best known were: Paget's *The Hope of the Katzekopfs* in 1844; Ruskin's *The King of the Golden*

River in 1851; Thackeray's *The Rose and the Ring,* in 1854; Kingsley's *The Heroes* in 1856 and *The Water Babies* in 1863; and Browne's *Granny's Wonderful Chair and Its Tales of Fairy Times* in 1857.

Thus a pattern of development can be traced in which previously rejected fairy tales became, toward the middle of the nineteenth century, almost the prevalent norm of canonized children's literature. When Nathaniel Hawthorne wished to adapt Greek mythology for children, he wrote to his publisher in 1851 that he would "aim at substituting a tone in some degree Gothic or romantic . . . instead of the classical coldness which is as repellant as the touch of marble" (Townsend 1977, 91–92). Yet Hawthorne's words reveal only one side of the struggle for what Townsend describes as "the rehabilitation" of fairy tales. This struggle, which began at the turn of the century with the triumph of those who fought against fairy tales (Sara Trimmer and her comrades), reached its peak in the bitter conflict between Dickens and Cruikshank. This conflict surfaced at the time of the revolutionary innovation in the children's system, when fairy tales first were being published (although in revised and moralized versions). In response to the publication of Cruikshank's version of *Hop-o'-My-Thumb,* Dickens published his attack on it, entitled "Frauds on the Fairies" (*Examiner,* 1 January 1853). As Steig claims, Cruikshank's book "was attacked vehemently by Charles Dickens, who in an *Examiner* article 'Frauds on the Fairies' argued for the importance of fairy-tales as 'nurseries of fancy,' and that 'whosoever alters them to suit his own opinions, whatever they are, is guilty . . . of an act of presumption, and appropriates to himself what does not belong to him'" (Steig 1980–81, 196). However, Cruikshank never fully understood why Dickens objected furiously to his adaptation; ten years later in 1864, when revising his original reply to "Frauds on the Fairies" for inclusion in *Puss in Boots,* Cruikshank wrote:

> And what are these doctrines and opinions [introduced into the fairy-tales]? Aye! What I have done? Where is the offence? Why, I have endeavoured to inculcate, at *the earliest age,* a *Horror of Drunkenness* and a recommendation of TOTAL ABSTINENCE from ALL INTOXICATING LIQUORS, which, if carried out universally, would not only do away with DRUNKENNESS ENTIRELY, but also with a large amount of POVERTY, MISERY, DISEASE, and DREADFUL CRIMES; also A DETESTATION OF

77

GAMBLING, and A LOVE OF ALL THAT IS VIRTUOUS AND GOOD, and an endeavour to impress on every one the *necessity, importance,* and *justice of every child* in the land receiving a usefule and religious education. And I would here ask in fairness, what harm can possibly be done to Fairy literature by such re-writing or editing as this? (Stone 1977–80, 245–46)

Dickens's crusade for unrevised fairy tales for children did not effect changes immediately. Despite the new attitude toward the previously forbidden fairy tales, their introduction into the children's system was permitted only on condition that they would be adjusted to the demands of the children's system. The attempt to meet these demands explains two dominant features, characteristic of early English fairy tales and fantasy stories for children.

In all fairy tales, a clear distinction was made between reality and fantasy. Fantasy was permissible only within very explicitly defined borders; thus writers considered it their duty to emphasize the imaginary nature of the text and the fact that it had no realistic ground. At the end of the eighteenth century, Mary Jane Kilner wrote in her foreword to *The Adventures of Pincushion:* "As I would not willingly mislead your judgment I would, previous to your reading this work, inform you that it is to be understood as an imaginary tale" (Townsend 1977, 47). Her words continued to echo in English children's literature for more than half a century.

Like any other canonized books for children, fairy tales that were written for the canonized system always had a moral. Gillian Avery states this when referring to mid nineteenth-century fairy tales:

All these early fairy tales have a strongly moral and didactic slant. None of the writers hesitates to use the conventions of fairyland for the purpose of teaching some useful lesson. . . . Enchantment in all these books, is only in the nature of supernatural machinery. There is no highly imaginative writing, no strange fairy tale settings, no original characterisation. Invariably the supernatural is used to point the moral, not because the writers feel an intrinsic interest in it." (1971, 323)

The moral had to suit the educational views of the time and thus had to demonstrate that the fairies for children encouraged the development of children's moral character. Cruikshank's adaptation of "Cinderella" that aroused Dickens's fury did this, yet was not such an exceptional example within the children's system of the time. Thus when the king proposed to celebrate the wedding of Cinderella and the prince by making the fountains flow with wine, the fairy godmother objects, arguing that the strong wine "leads also to quarrels, brutal fights and violent deaths. . . . The history of the use of strong drinks . . . is marked on every page by excess, which follows, as a matter of course, from the very nature of their composition, and [is] always accompanied by ill-health, misery and crime" (Stone 1977–80, 240). Consequently, the king "gave orders that all the wine, beer and spirits in the place should be collected together . . . and made a great bonfire on the night of the wedding" (Townsend 1977, 92). Thus, despite the fact that writers (mainly of the mainstream writing for adults) began to oppose the demands concerning children's literature in general (the demand for a moral), and fantasy in particular, writing for children still had to obey these demands if it wished to be accepted by the children's system.

CARROLL'S MANIPULATION OF EXISTING MODELS

A historical overview of English literature shows quite clearly that *Alice* was not the first children's fantasy story and thus could not possibly have gained its status as a "classic" (a text of great importance) merely because it was a fantasy story. *Alice* was considered a turning point already in its own time, as well as in several historiographies (see Darton 1958, Townsend 1977, Muir 1969), not because of the introduction of the fantasy model, but because of the way the fantasy model was handled. It was Carroll's manipulation of the existing model of the fantasy story, as well as other prevailing models in English literature of the time, that created a new model; making the text a classic and a subject for imitation.

Carroll very quickly became a model for imitation and several writers admitted their indebtedness to him, as did the Australian writer of *Bertie and Bullfrogs*, who wrote the following author's apology to Lewis Carroll:

Dreamer of fancies thoughtful, quaint and tender,
Wonderer of wonders so grotesquely bold,
Lord of Misrule, of Nonsense sworn Defender,
Reducing to madcap laughter young and old,
Pardon a humble follower whose hand
Plucks this poor twig from out thy crown of laurel
To plant it in the fair Australian land,
And grow inspired by thee, a Christmas Carroll.

(Saxby 1969)

Historically speaking, *Alice* is very similar to Gogol's "The Nose" in its handling of existing models. Gogol used models existing in several systems, literary and non-literary, and manipulated them in several ways in order to produce a new model; moreover, he produced a new model that was developed through the manipulation of several existing models and was based on the distortion of already existing models (see Vinogradov 1922). Historically, it is not its position as a totally new and previously unknown model that makes the text a "masterpiece" or warrants its consideration as a "turning point," but rather it is the manipulation of models already existing in the system that earns status for the text. However, the procedure, which is typical of the adult system, is more difficult to maintain in children's literature because of the system's strong tendency of self-perpetuation. Still, in the case of *Alice*, it was the ambivalent character of the text that liberated Carroll from the limitations imposed on children's literature (particularly on children's fantasy) and gave him the freedom to produce a text based on a different model of fantasy.

CHARACTERISTICS OF *ALICE'S ADVENTURES IN WONDERLAND*
AS AN AMBIVALENT TEXT

My discussion of *Alice* does not propose to offer an exhaustive interpretation of the text, nor a detailed description of its characteristic features. It is mainly aimed at exploring structural features that endow the different versions with ambivalent character. This requires discussion of Carroll's handling of models current at the time, especially as far as the level of moral, parody, and relations between fantasy and reality are concerned.

The text is based on three different models that existed in children's literature at the time. Carroll combined these models and, in doing so, distorted and altered them. He combined two prominent models of children's literature—that of the adventure story and that of the fantasy story—and added them to the model of a nonsense story (Lear's famous *Book of Nonsense* was first published in 1846). The first model had been prominent in children's literature in the preceding fifty years, while the latter two were gaining recognition. Carroll himself seemed to have been aware of the novelty of his text (because of the change in the conventional model). In his diary he later wrote: "That was many a year ago, but I distinctly remember now, as I write, how, *in a desperate attempt to strike out some new line of fairy lore*, I had sent my heroine straight down a rabbit-hole" (Carroll [1887] 1961, 165, my italics). In a letter to a friend he declared "I can guarantee that the books have no religious teaching whatever in them—in fact they do not teach anything at all" (Green 1960, 51). This was quite a provocative declaration at the time and certainly indicated a new concept of children's literature. Thus Carroll abandoned the moral level, which was still considered mandatory in children's literature (though no longer in adult literature). In this respect, he violated an almost sacred rule of current canonized children's literature; nevertheless, this violation was made possible thanks to adult acceptance of the book.

Ironically, in Carroll's time children liked the book precisely because of its lack of moral. Lord Bertrand Russell, in answering a question on whether children today still read *Alice*, replied: "My experience . . . is that they don't, and I think this because there are so many more children's books now and because when I was young, it was the only children's book that hadn't got a moral. We all got very tired of morals in books" (Gardner 1969, 151–52). As Green claims, the lack of moral in itself signaled the novelty of the text, though modern norms of writing for children make it difficult to grasp this: "*Alice* is so much a part of the cultural heritage of the Western World that it is hard to realize its uniqueness or to see how startlingly new it was. . . . To see how utterly different it was from all that had gone before, one has but to read *The Water Babies* (1863), an absolute orgy of self-conscious didacticism" (Green 1960, 52). However, it was not only the lack of a moral in the text that made children so enthusiastic, but also the option the text left them to realize only the more established models and to ignore the parody on those models (parody that appealed to adults). Thus, in *Alice*, Carroll parodied various elements of several established models of children's literature, although his main target was the popular children's verses of the time, written during the eighteenth century and the beginning of the nineteenth. In fact, those verses were the literary heritage of the tradition on which Carroll and his contemporaries had grown up. In his annotated *Alice*, Gardner even claims: "Most of the poems in the two Alice books are parodies of poems or popular songs that were well known to Carroll's contemporary readers" (1977, 38). For instance, Carroll parodied two poems that had strong moralistic emphasis. When Alice sings, "You are old, Father William," her verse is a parody of the didactic poem "The Old Man's Comforts and How He Gained Them" by Robert Southey (1774–1843). In another case, "How doth the little crocodile / Improve his shining tail," Carroll made a parody of one of the best-known poems (of a strong moralistic slant) by Isaac Watt (1674–1748)—"Against Idleness and Mischief," which was undoubtedly part of the heritage of English children's literature of that time.

Parody, as Tynjanov (1971) argued, is typical when norms change in the literary system and indicates the approaching end of a literary period. In the parody, the writer bases the new model on the remodeling of an already exiting model, thus introducing the established model (while abusing it at the same time), or as Erlich explained it: "This is, the Formalist critic implies, how literary change comes about. The old is presented, as it were, in a new key. The obsolete device is not thrown overboard, but repeated in a new incongruous context, and thus either rendered absurd through the agency of mechanization or made 'perceptible' again" (1969, 258). Parody, no doubt, contributes to the nonsense level of the text, but its more important function is linked with Carroll's endeavor to break the prevailing norms in children's literature. Once mocked, it becomes difficult for the parodied texts to be accepted again. Carroll's manipulation of existing models resulted in the production of a new model that served as a prototype of children's books to follow. As MacCann claimed: "*Alice* set a precedent in children's books. The influence of such imaginative and irreverent story-telling opened the

way for the development of the fantastic genre in children's literature" (1969, 133). This new "fantastic" genre was created when
Carroll brought into the model of the fantasy story elements of the
adventure and nonsense stories. On the whole, he did not change the
existing fantastic model by deleting elements, but rather by changing
their functions. As a result, motivation for the introduction of various
elements changed, as did their hierarchy, especially in regarding the
rules of space and time and the relations between reality and fantasy.

While children's literature was keen to distinguish between reality
and fantasy, even after imagination had been as Townsend says "rehabilitated," Carroll deliberately blurred relations between fantasy
and reality. This diffusion is made possible by the nature of the difference between fantasy and reality. This difference is not the result
of presenting different elements but the result of their different organization, which creates different fields of reference (see Hrushovski
1979). Hence, the same elements can participate in different fields of
reference to create different worlds based on different models of organization: in one, a world organized in a fantastic field of reference;
in the other, a world organized in a realistic field of reference.

In fact, *Alice* manipulates the various fields of reference in order
to obscure the differences between fantasy and reality. This manipulation makes it possible for the same elements to appear at first in a
dream (or something that at least can be partly explained as a dream)
and immediately afterward to be dreamt about as if they had occurred in reality. The same elements take part in both occurrences;
only the dimensions through which they are seen are different.

Fantasy is then described by Carroll in terms of a real occurrence
and vice versa, and therefore it is very difficult to distinguish between
what happens in reality and what happens as fantasy. If the confused
relations between fantasy and reality at two decisive points of the
text—the beginning and the end—are analyzed, it will be observed
that, in both cases, it is impossible to label definitively either of the
episodes as a dream or as a real event.

The opening scene sets a pastoral view where the rabbit that
passes by could be part of the setting and the bored girl could be
asleep and dreaming. In this case, the whole story could have been
motivated as a dream and the transition from the white rabbit to the
talking white rabbit could have been explained as a transition from

reality to a dream. Carroll builds this option but at the same time seems to cancel it because he does not leave anything determined and final. Thus, Alice is not asleep, but rather tired and sleepy; moreover, the option to see the rabbit as part of the setting (the shores of the bank) is built in one paragraph only to be canceled in the next:

> Alice was beginning to get very tired of sitting by her sister on the bank, and of having nothing to do. . . .
> So she was considering, in her own mind (as well as she could, for the hot day made her feel very sleepy and stupid), whether the pleasure of making a daisy-chain would be worth the trouble of getting up and picking the daisies, when suddenly a white rabbit with pink eyes ran close by her. (Gardner 1977, 25)

Carroll not only draws from the option (which was already built in the text) of seeing the white rabbit as part of the setting, but he is also keen to draw attention to the rabbit's appearance by having Alice comment on it, thus "making strange" the dual existence of the elements mentioned: "There was nothing so *very* remarkable in that; nor did Alice think it so *very* much out of the way to hear the Rabbit say to itself, 'Oh dear! Oh dear! I shall be too late!' (when she thought it over afterwards, it occurred to her that she ought to have wondered at this, but at the time it all seemed quite natural)" (Gardner 1977, 25–26). Moreover, Carroll uses the order of events introduced in order to make us accept the situation; only then does he point to the abnormality of the entire situation. Alice does not marvel at the rabbit talking to himself, but she does marvel at the rabbit taking out his watch. Of course, both acts of the rabbit are equally strange. The fact that Alice marvels at only one of them not only draws attention to the peculiar situation but to the possible world built into the text as well (Pavel 1976). The meta-text technique—"when she thought it over afterwards, it occurred to her that she ought to have wondered at this,"—not only gives legitimation to a reconstruction of the situation, but also calls attention to the world presented in the text. This is a possible world with its own rules which are so coherent that they might mislead us to believe that they are really valid and possible. Carroll first makes us believe them to be possible; only later does he occasionally digress from this presentation and calls for a comparison between the "real" world and the possible world.

On the other hand, Carroll deliberately confuses the two worlds— and in the most decisive points of the text; that is, he does it not only at the beginning of the story, but at the end as well. For example, Alice grows back to her normal size when she is still with the cards. In other words, she comes back to the "real" world when she is still in the possible world of fantasy. This confusion of the two worlds is described in detail as a long process, hence making the coexistence of the two worlds endure for quite a long time:

> "If any one of them can explain it," said Alice, (she had grown so large in the last few minutes that she wasn't a bit afraid of interrupting him). . . .
> "Who cares for *you?*" said Alice (she had grown to her full size by this time). "You're nothing but a pack of cards!" (Gardner 1977, 159, 161)

To make matters even more confused, Carroll does not end the story when Alice wakes up; rather, he leaves the question of whether or not it was a dream open, and even makes Alice's sister dream the whole story again. Thus, while he opened the story by framing it into another story, he uses the sister's dream to reframe the entire text into "a dream within a dream": "But her sister sat still just as she left her, leaning her head on her hand, watching the setting sun, and thinking of little Alice and all her wonderful Adventures, till she too began dreaming after a fashion, and this was her dream . . ." (Gardner 1977, 162).

This complicated technique totally blurs relations between the two worlds. Alice's sister dreams about Alice's adventures, as if they were of real substance, whose existence equals that of the real world. In such a way, Carroll questions the boundaries between the two dimensions. If a dream can be dreamed about, as if it were real, conversely, reality can be described as if it were a dream. The two dimensions exist equally and are equally "real." Evidence of this can be seen when Alice's sister dreams about Alice and about her adventures in the same sequence, without distinguishing between them at all:

The long grass rustled at her feet as the White Rabbit hurried by—the frightened Mouse splashed his way through the neighbouring pool—she could hear the rattle of the teacups as the March Hare and his friends shared their never-ending meal, and the shrill voice of the Queen ordering off her unfortunate guests to execution—once more the pig-baby was sneezing on the Duchess's knee, while plates and dishes crashed around it—once more the shriek of the Gryphon, the squeaking of the Lizard's slate-pencil, and the choking of the suppressed guinea-pigs, filled the air, mixed up with the distant sob of the miserable Mock Turtle.

So she sat on, with closed eyes, and half believed herself in Wonderland, though she knew she had but to open them again, and all would change to dull reality—the grass would be only rustling in the wind, and the pool rippling to the waving of the reeds—the rattling teacups would change to tinkling sheep-bells, and the Queen's shrill cries to the voice of the shepherd boy—and the sneeze of the baby, the shriek of the Gryphon, and all the other queer noises, would change (she knew) to the confused clamour of the busy farm-yard—while the lowing of the cattle in the distance would take the place of the Mock Turtle's heavy sobs. (Gardner 1977, 163–64)

The blurred distinction between real and unreal and the transition from one to another can be "explained" only in accordance with the conventions of a nonsense story, where motivation other than the logical is permitted. Thus, the transition from reality to fantasy and vice versa cannot be logically explained (unless the internal "logic" of the story is accepted). The same rule holds true for the description of space and time in the text. The text sets its own code for the time and space, and builds them accordingly. Thus, the transition from one space to another is not based on a realistic model, but more often than not on metonymic relations. Alice, for instance, is at one moment inside a room, then the room becomes a small pool (the pool of tears), and later the pool becomes part of the outside world. Again, Carroll emphasizes the peculiar transition by having the transition based on a realistic model canceled. Alice cannot get out through the door:

And she ran with all speed back to the little door; but alas! the little door was shut again, and the little golden key was lying on the glass table as before. (Gardner, 1977, 39)

> As she said these words her foot slipped, and in another moment, splash! she was up to her chin in salt water. . . . However, she soon made out that she was in the pool of tears which she had wept. (40)
> Just then she heard something splashing about in the pool a little way off. (41)
> Alice led the way, and the whole party swam to the shore. (44)

The fact that Carroll suggests several options and then draws back from them, does not cancel them, because once presented, they are built into the text (see Perry 1979). Usually those options (canceled later) that are part of the more established model allow Carroll (despite the distortion) to leave open the choice of reading the text either as a simple fantasy story or even as a simple adventure story. The reader, in a sense, can realize only the well-known established elements and thus can construct the established model only.

Carroll's other versions, especially *The Nursery Alice*, support the view that the features described above (such as a blurred distinction between reality and imagination, spatial transitions) are characteristic of the ambivalent text and, in fact, contribute to its ambivalent nature. When Carroll (as well as the translators/adaptors) adapted the text for children, he totally omitted the features described above, and instead, acted as follows. First, Carroll totally changed the tone of the text. He adjusted it to the condescending authoritative tone, which was typical of conventional didactic stories of the time, and especially to those intended to be read *to* children and not *by* children. This tone has nothing whatsoever to do with Alice Liddell, as is often suggested, who was thirty-seven when *The Nursery Alice* was published. Rather, it has to do with the conventional tone of children's books at the time, of which Carroll was undoubtedly aware, for he maintained a similar tone in his intentionally didactic story of *Sylvie and Bruno*. In *The Nursery Alice*, Carroll says: "You'll never guess what it was: so I shall have to tell you" (Carroll 1966, 7). The second action Carroll took was the omission of all the elements of satire or parody. This is very obvious in the case of the systematically omitted poems. The satirical poems, which had mainly contributed to the parody level, were left functionless in a version meant for children only. Finally, Carroll made *Alice* a simple fantasy story, based on the conventional model of the time. The distorted relations between space and time, fantasy and reality, were restored since Carroll was eager to distinguish between reality and fantasy and thus no confusion was permissible. In each of the texts the author manipulates the relationship bewteen time and space on the one hand, and reality and fantasy on the other. In *Alice's Adventures in Wonderland,* Alice's fall into the rabbit hole takes a long time, more than realistically possible according to the laws of gravitation. The sense of this continuous fall is created by Carroll's special manipulation of time and space. By combining elements of both, Carroll described time in terms of space, changing the rules of time. Carroll emphasizes the continuous fall by having Alice pick up a jar of marmalade. The passing time is then described by the elements of space—the shelves: "She took down a jar from one of the shelves as she passed: it was labeled 'ORANGE MARMALADE' but to her great disappointment it was empty" (Gardner 1977, 27). Alice even finds time to put the marmalade back on the shelves, an act that reinforces the sense of the slowly passing time: "So [she] managed to put it into one of the cupboards as she fell past it" (Gardner 1977, 27).

On the other hand, the peculiar sense of space (which by itself is used for describing time) is created by Carroll's special motivation of spatial elements, which deviates from conventional presentation. Carroll does not base his description on realistic models, but on metonymic relations, and more specifically, metonymic transfers from one element to another, which are impossible or unthinkable in terms of realistic models. Carroll uses metonymic transfer in the description of the space of the rabbit hole, which suddenly turns into a well; thus the transfer from one space to another is deliberately confused. In realistic terms, this transformation could not have been possible. There simply was no room for any of the mentioned spatial elements except for grass and stone. Yet Carroll manages to create a description that allows for such transformation and for the mentioning of certain items such as shelves without ever provoking the reader to notice or question it. He does this in spite of the fact that the description lacks any realistic basis and is actually based on metonymic relations. Once Alice is underground, it is the underground that enables the transition from the hole into a well. Moreover, once the shelves decorating the well are mentioned, they supply the motivation for the introduction of other elements that, in terms of realistic models, represent different spaces (marmalade jar—the kitchen; maps—the classroom): "Then she looked at the sides of the well, and noticed that they were filled with cupboards and bookshelves: here and there she saw maps and pictures hung on pegs" (Gardner 1977, 26–27). However, when Carroll (and his translators) extricated the text from its ambivalent status (in *The Nursery Alice*), he deleted the sophisticated handling of space and time and motivated the description of the fall on a different basis than in *Alice's Adventures in Wonderland* (either on a model of a dream or on a realistic model).

Thus Carroll gives a rational explanation for the fall in *The Nursery Alice*, declaring that such a long fall is possible in terms of a dream: "If anybody *really* had such a long fall as that, it would kill them, most likely: but you know it doesn't hurt a bit to fall in a *dream*, because all the time you *think* you're falling, you really *are* lying somewhere, safe and sound, and fast asleep!" (*The Nursery Alice*, 3). Carroll also deleted all the spatial description of the well and described it as a rabbit hole, emphasizing both the difference and similarity between a well and a rabbit hole:

> . . . and she ran, and she ran, till she tumbled right down the rabbit-hole.
> . . . It was just like a very deep well: only there was no water in it.
> (*The Nursery Alice*, 3)

Writers who adapted *Alice's Adventures in Wonderland* for children were also not happy with Carroll's manipulation of time and space and relations between reality and fantasy. They acted, from a point of principle, precisely as Carroll did in *The Nursery Alice*, probably without even being aware of this version's existence. Their similar adaptations, in fact, might well reveal more than anything else those elements that needed reformulation; only through their and Carroll's reformulations could the text lose its ambivalent status and regain the univalent one considered appropriate for children.

Just like Carroll, adaptors felt it was necessary to withdraw from the blurred relations between reality and fantasy. Therefore they motivated the first scene in either realistic or dream terms, usually making the fall very short and realistically possible. The Disney edition shows this change:

Alice was growing tired, listening to her sister read. Just as her eyes began to close, she saw a white rabbit hurry by, looking at his pocket watch and talking to himself. Alice thought that was very curious indeed—a talking rabbit with a pocket watch! So she followed him into a rabbit hole beneath a big tree.

And down she fell, down to the center of the world, it seemed.

When Alice landed with a thump . . . (Disney 1980)

In the Octopus edition a similar adjustment was made: "She followed him [the rabbit] down a large rabbit hole. At the bottom she found a small table and a tiny key" (Octopus 1980). The Modern Promotions edition also followed suit:

So she fell asleep, and this is what she dreamed.

All at once, a White Rabbit came running by. . . . Alice wanted to see what would happen to it; so she ran and ran, till she found herself tumbling down through a rabbit-hole after it.

After Alice had run a long long way underground, suddenly she entered a great hall with many doors. (Modern Promotions)

In the Modern Promotions adaptation the writer used as a motivation both the dream and the realistic explanation, though he carefully separated the two—Alice is dreaming the whole scene ("that is what she dreamed"), but still the space is a rabbit hole. Moreover, she does not fall at all, but rather runs through the hole.

Concomitantly, fantasy is motivated in the *Nursery* version as something that happens in a dream; a logical explanation exists for each event. When Alice wakes up she finds "that the cards were only some leaves off the tree, that the wind had blown down upon her face" (Carroll 1966, 56). Furthermore, Carroll bothers to emphasize again that the whole story is a dream: "*Wouldn't* it be a nice thing to have a curious dream, just like Alice?" (Carroll 1966, 56). Again, translators acted as Carroll did, and explained the whole story as a dream:

At this the whole pack flew up into the air.

Alice tried to brush them away—and found that they were only wind-blown leaves brushing her face. She was awake once more, and her sister was smiling at her. "Oh, I've had such a curious dream!" she said.

Wouldn't you like to have a wonderful dream, too, just like Alice? (Modern Promotions)

She covered her eyes with her hands and when she took them away she found she was in her own garden at home. All her adventures in Wonderland had been just a dream. (Octopus 1980)

The difference between the two versions, the opposition between the tones, the lack of parody and satire in the *Nursery* version, and the different handling of space and time and the relations between reality and fantasy all indicate how well Carroll was aware of his implied reader each time. This awareness of potential readers and potential realizations of the text seem to be among the reasons for Carroll's decision to produce both an ambivalent and univalent text. Though the ambivalent version is seldom read by children today, it was a text that initiated new options for children's writers and became a model for imitation for many later children's books.

Texts

ENGLISH EDITIONS

Carroll, Lewis. [1865] 1968. *Alice's Adventures in Wonderland.* New York: MacMillan.
———. [1886] 1965. *Alice's Adventures Underground.* New York: Dover.
———. [1890] 1966. *The Nursery Alice.* New York: Dover.

ENGLISH ADAPTATIONS

Alice in Wonderland Coloring Book. 1972. New York: Dover.
Alice's Adventures in Wonderland. New York: Modern Promotions.
Alice in Wonderland. 1980. London: Octopus.
Disney, Walt. 1980. *Alice in Wonderland.* Adapted by Al Dempster. Racine, Wis.: Golden Press.

HEBREW TRANSLATIONS

Carroll, Lewis. 1945. *Alisa be'eretz ha-plaot.* Translated by Avraham Aryeh Akavya. Tel Aviv: Sreberk.

——. 1973. *Alisa be'eretz ha-plaot.* Translated by Bela Bar'am. Tel Aviv: Massada.

——. 1976. *Alisa be'eretz ha-plaot.* Translated by Shulamit Lapid. Tel Aviv: Yavneh.

Chapter Four

Adults and Children
in Non-Canonized Children's Literature

 As discussed earlier, children's literature is subject to systemic constraints that are imposed on the texts and to a large extent determine their characterization and presentation. One of the most powerful constraints is the special and often ambiguous status of the addressee in a children's book, since it must appeal to the child reader and the adult, who is regarded in culture both as superior to the child and as responsible for deciding what is appropriate reading material for the child. This tendency has developed because our present culture, or at least the establishment involved in the production of children's books, attach great importance to the child's reading material as crucial for his development and his mental welfare. Hence the phenomenon of institutionalized and noninstitutionalized censorship of children's books has developed, which has the power to banish or accept a children's book (see the dominance of censorship over children's books in America, discussed in Stein 1975 and Donelson 1976). As a result, those people whose goal is to guide and direct children's reading—teachers, librarians, and parents—are overwhelmed by periodicals evaluating children's literature.

This forces the children's writer to compromise between two addressees who differ both in their literary tastes as well as in their norms of realization of the text. The writer must skillfully craft this compromise, employing a complicated range of "compensation strategies" while remaining within the limits of the system's prevalent norms, in order to reach both addressees. While most writers appeal to both addresses in their works, others use either the ambivalent text, discussed in the previous chapter, or non-canonized children's literature, discussed in this chapter, as solutions to the addressee dilemma.

Although the two solutions normally stand at extreme poles on the axis of norms of writing for children, they do share one common denominator: in both, the writer manages to ignore one of his addressees. In an ambivalent text he uses the child as a "pseudo-addressee" (by officially addressing the text to him, but primarily and practically addressing it to adults). In popular literature he ignores the adult and rejects the need to court him and obtain his approval. The result of the second approach is usually the rejection of the text by the "people in culture" who will probably impose various restrictions on the text. In most cases, they will attempt to prevent its being read by children; in extreme cases, they might banish it from the library or even burn it (see Davis 1976). One consequence is certain: the book will not be recommended by teachers and librarians. In fact, they will do their best to boycott its purchase and hence threaten its commercial prospects.

Faced with these consequences, why are writers for children ready to take the risk? This question is even more crucial when the main movitation for writing and publishing popular literature is recognized as the opportunity not to gain status and recognition (the chances of that are poor) but rather to achieve commercial success. Interestingly enough, these condemned books do eventually manage to succeed commercially. As a matter of fact, they are sometimes extremely successful. Surveys of reading habits and publishers' reports show that the more lowly regarded writers are, the better their books sell (Enid Blyton's books and the Nancy Drew series illustrate the matter; see Donelson 1978 and Whitehead 1977). How is this possible? How do the condemned texts manage to overcome the boycott and sell so well? The answer for this seeming paradox involves many factors, not all of which can be discussed here. My aim is simply to focus on the textual features which, in my view, are responsible for this success. However, the boycott imposed on these books ironically only increases their sales, for it forces children willing to read them to buy them—they are not in the local library. Obviously, this is not the main reason for their huge success. Rather, their great appeal to such a huge audience has to do with the stereotypical plots and characterization common to any popular literature (see Kreuzer 1967,

Even-Zohar 1978a). In the case of children's literature, the stereotypical presentation involves the *text's portrayal of a children's world in which adults hardly exist at all*. In fact, this portrayal is one of the manifestations of the writer's ignoring of the adult reader. Moreover, popular literature for children not only tends to ignore adults, but also to create an opposition between two worlds, based on deictic oppositions (an opposition between two territorial dimensions and/or two dimensions of time, suggesting an uncompromising boundary between children and adults).

Thus, the text offers a world that excludes adults; even if adults are present, they are subject to negative evaluation. Of course, the portrayal of a children's world in which adults do not take part is also typical of canonized children's literature.[1] There are quite a few canonized texts for children where not only "orphaning" of children occurs, but a total separation between children and adults takes place.

In this respect, the difference between canonized and non-canonized children's literature lies in their attitude toward the adult world. While canonized children's literature takes the codex of the adult world as a model for imitation, non-canonized children's literature tries to challenge and to create the impression of a new codex, typical of children only. Indeed, it is usually no more than impression, because the new codex imitates that of the adults in many respects. However, while in canonized literature the separation is only physical, non-canonized literature does try to create a mental separation, but not always with much success. The two opposing worlds of adults and children in non-canonized children's literature will be explored here by analyzing a sample of Enid Blyton's texts (as well as some remarks on the parallel American case of the Nancy Drew series).

Enid Blyton was chosen primarily because she was both prolific (writing about six hundred books) and popular (selling millions of copies, Stoney 1974). Her books were translated into many languages and published in many countries, including the United States

---

[1] The handling of adults and children in canonized children's literature is also very different from adult literature, which uses similar subjects mainly for allegorical purposes. For instance, Richard Hughes's *A High Wind in Jamaica* describes children as little murderers, which would never be acceptable in children's literature.

(which is unusual, as American children's literature tends to translate very little, and if it does, mostly "classic" texts). Some of Blyton's books were even made into a television series. In short, Blyton's success is beyond doubt and by no means accidental; consequently, her case is of significance. In addition, it is my belief that characteristics in Blyton's books are also typical to less prominent popular literature. For similar reasons, the parallel American case of the Nancy Drew series is an ideal model for investigation (for a more detailed analysis of the Nancy Drew series, see Donelson 1978). Written over the course of fifty years (since 1930) by several ghost writers (mainly by Harriet Adams) under the pseudonym of Carolyn Keene, the books of the Nancy Drew series have also sold millions of copies. At the same time, the series has also been one of the most defamed in the United States.

In addition to the parallel success and "low esteem," the Nancy Drew series resembles Blyton's books (in spite of obvious differences) as far as the main issues of portrayal of the relationship between adults and children is concerned. The fact that the two series differ in prominent respects, such as the hero's age (children versus adolescents) and the structure of the plot (one plot versus two parallel intersecting plots), should not prevent the observance of the overall similarity between them in one of the most important issues. The two series face similar problems and offer similar solutions in handling the relationship between adults and children, while maintaining and advancing middle-class values. Nevertheless, my discussion will focus on Enid Blyton's texts, as they prove to be an ideal test case for quite a few kinds of national popular children's literatures.

A Test Case: Enid Blyton's Works

CHARACTERIZATION OF CHILDREN AND ADULTS: SOME PROBLEMS AND SOLUTIONS

How does Blyton portray children? Whether it is the Four, the Five, the Seven, or any mystery, the same portrayal of children repeats itself: a group of children of well-to-do families are involved (mostly during their vacation) in some adventure or mystery that they manage to solve without adult help. Only toward the end of the story do they bring it to the attention of their parents or the police (or both), at which time they are highly praised by those adults. Deviations from this structure were found to be slight and insignificant, after sampling eighteen books that were picked at random and checked carefully.

This portrayal of children posed some difficulties for Blyton, especially as far as the relations between adults and children are concerned in regard to the values of the texts. Blyton portrays middle-class children whose values the text does not violate, but rather accepts and even reinforces (for a similar problem, see Neuschäfer 1971). How then is it possible to maintain middle-class values that assume both the dominant position of parents in the hierarchical family structure and the children's obedience and at the same time that create two opposing worlds between children and adults? The answer to this conflict involves the sophisticated presentation of adults and a varied range of devices used to create an exclusive world for children.

Adults as described by Blyton fall into three different categories in regard to their presentation in the text and the extent of their involvement in the adventure (these categories also overlap with their social standing, their physical description, and consequently, their evaluation by the text). Thus, during the adventure adults surrounding children either hardly take part, disturb the children and almost prevent them from solving the mystery, or constitute the criminals against whom the children fight.

In Nancy Drew books, this pattern is slightly different, not only because Nancy is much older than Blyton's children, but mainly because she is not part of a group of children. Still, in most cases Nancy manages to solve the mystery with the help of her girlfriends, Bess and George (George, by the way, is a boyish-looking girl who bears a most striking similarity to Blyton's George). In some cases, she is also assisted by her boyfriends, Ned and Dave. However, Nancy shares with her English counterpart a high social standing, good manners, and of course an uncanny ability to solve mysteries.

RELATIONS BETWEEN CHILDREN AND THEIR PARENTS

Blyton's texts emphasize the good manners and education of her middle-class children. Children of other classes rarely enter the scene; if they do, the text repeatedly stresses their inferior status. This occurs in the text's unflattering description of the gypsy girl, who will never be like the children of the Five:

> She had been taught to clean her teeth and wash and do her hair. . . .
> . . . but all that was forgotten now that she was leading a gypsy life again!
> "In a day or two she'll be the filthy, dirty, tangly-haired, rude girl she was when we just knew her," said George, combing out *her own hair extra well.* (*Five Have a Wonderful Time,* 100, my italics)

On the other hand, the text always emphasizes the good manners of the children:

> Julian stood up *politely.* (*Five on Finniston Farm,* 36, my italics)
> "We like talking to Janie," said Julian *politely.* (76, my italics)

The Nancy Drew texts take her good manners for granted; hence it is necessary to account for any seeming deviation from it. For instance, when Nancy is eager to read a letter she has just received, the text remarks: "A letter from Europe was something she did not often receive, and she was tempted to be impolite enough to discover its secret" (*Nancy's Mysterious Letter,* 7); or when she reads a letter that was not addressed to her, the following explanation is given: "Nancy had been taught that mail is a personal thing and unless specific permission is given, it is to be left strictly unread by anyone but the addressee" (*Nancy's Mysterious Letter,* 167). The presentation of children as well-mannered, middle-class children made it impossible to create a clash between parents and children. A clash of this sort might cause inconsistency in the values of the text and blur its clear-cut values, which do not allow for a complicated value system. On the other hand, a clash with parents seems to be inevitable once the children begin their adventure by themselves. Skillfully Blyton managed to avoid the clash with parents by utilizing the following three devices: parents are "heard but not seen"; parents are replaced by substitutes with whom a clash is not only permitted, but advisable; when the text portrays a clash between child and parent (or relative), the parent eventually turns out to be a false one, making the child only serve as an alibi for some devious intention of the false parent.

The device of parents "heard but not seen" is very common. In some books, Blyton simply gets rid of parents by sending them away. Either the children are on vacation or the parents are on vacation or both, and they communicate via the telephone or letters. When this trick is worn out, Blyton's parents become too ill for the children to see; she even goes as far as sending parents to a hospital. For instance, in *The Secret Seven,* the mother is just going to a meeting: "I think Mummy's going out tonight, so it should be all right" (*The Secret Seven,* 65). In *Five Are Together Again,* the children cannot get near the parents: "You see, neither your uncle nor I have had scarlet fever—so we are in quarantine, and mustn't have anyone near us" (13). Meanwhile, in *Five Run Away Together,* George's mother is taken to a hospital: "Your mother was suddenly taken very ill . . . and they've taken her away to hospital and your father went with her" (32). Nevertheless, not always such a drastic removal of parents is required. In quite a few texts, parents do exist somewhere in the background, but they rarely participate in the scenes (sometimes not even in the dialogues and almost never in the adventures themselves). Their absence is accounted for by standard societal expectations: fathers are at work, hence, no problems raised; mothers are attending some meeting or giving a little party, so obviously, children must be kept away (the territorial boundaries of children are discussed later).

The absence of parents from dialogues (much of the texts is devoted to dialogues) is not so total and systematic as their absence from the actual adventure. Dialogues in which parents participate do occur, but quite often the parent's speech is reported or given in embedded speech or the parent speaks to the child from behind, thus achieving his actual absence from the scene. For instance, in *The Secret Seven,* mother does take part in the dialogue, but she is not to be seen:

"Janet, Janet, what's the matter, dear? What's happened?"
"Oh—nothing, Mummy," called back Janet, *suddenly remembering that this was Secret Society business.* (38, my italics)

In the same book Peter reports that *"Mummy said* we could go out; it's a nice sunny morning" (10, my italics), while in another case the child's speech is given in direct speech but the mother's in embedded speech: " 'Will she be able to come and see us tomorrow morning?' He asked Barbara's mother, and *she said yes, she thought so*" (10, my italics). In Nancy Drew books, an even less complicated solution was offered: Nancy's mother died when the girl was very young. Her substitute, Hannah Gruen, is very kind, though her low social position precludes the possibility that she takes part in the adventure. Nancy's father, on the other hand, supports his daughter, appreciates her talent, and even asks her for help. But even he seldom participates in the adventure. The text always manages to find an excuse to exclude him from it, as is plainly evident in the following episode: "Nancy knew, even before she opened it, what the envelope contained. She had often found such messages from her parent, and always they contained the same announcement: '—an unexpected call out of town. I will not be home for two or three days' " (*Nancy's Mysterious Letter*, 91). Either Nancy goes on vacation, or her father goes away, or both are away; still they continue to communicate by telephone, even at the expense of long-distance calls (as they do in *The Mystery of the Brass Bound Trunk*). However, as in Blyton's books, Nancy's father physically exists in most cases only at the beginning of the adventure or when it reaches its climax. In such a way, the texts manage to reinforce the actual existence of children and minimize the presence of parents whose existence they cannot cancel altogether.

Middle-class ethos is also maintained by the text's emphasis on the children's attitude toward their parents and on their good manners. The children are always polite to their parents, respect them dearly, and usually maintain ideal relationships, as is evident from the following description of Nancy Drew's father: "Carson Drew was a tall, distinguished-looking man of middle age, with keen, twinkling blue eyes like those of his daughter. He and his only child were good companions and shared a delightful sense of humour" (*The Ghost of Blackwood Hall*, 20). In contrast, the attitude of Blyton's children toward their parents is emphasized by the fact that they always obey their parents' orders. Moreover, the texts stress their obedience in a typical English manner: they are never late for their meals unless they have some extraordinary reasons! (In *Five on Finniston Farm*, they are trapped underground and thus cannot come to tea on time—a lesser excuse than that will not do.)

SUBSTITUTES AND PSEUDO-PARENTS

The children's respectful attitude toward their parents is especially prominent when compared to their attitude toward pseudo-parents or substitutes. The only real father with whom a clash occurs is George's father in the Five. But, take note: the seeming clash with George's father is "justified" by his characterization as a volatile genius and by the knowledge that it is only a temporary conflict. As a matter of fact, George's father loves her, understands her, and only wants her to have the best: "He was a very clever and hard-working scientist, impatient, hot-tempered, kindly and very forgetful. How he wished his daughter was not so exactly like him" (*Five Have a Wonderful Time*, 13). However, in all other cases the conflict is with a pseudo-parent. It is either a stepfather (like Mr. Andrews in *Five Go to Smugglers' Top*) or a pseudo-relative, who takes the child under his care after the death of the child's parents, mainly in order to use the child for criminal purposes (such as Martin Corton's father in *Five on Kirrin Island Again* or Novie's uncle in *Five Go Off in a Caravan*).

For fear of contradicting the middle-class ethos, Blyton had to avoid any clash with parents. But she did need some kind of conflict between children and adults to create two opposing worlds. To do this, Blyton compensates for her handling of parents by justifying confrontation with other adults who populate the texts. The first and most important compensation is given in the form of a parent-substitute whom the texts very often portray as the source of conflict with the children. There might be a very simple conflict with one's nurse (Miss Ely in *The Secret Seven*) or a very serious one, as in *Five Run Away Together* or *Five Go Adventuring Again*. In *Five Run Away Together*, the substitute is the Stick family, requested by George's father to take care of the children when her mother is taken to the hospital (George's father forces the children to obey them: "Surely you children can see to yourselves and make do with Mrs. Stick till I get back!" [40]). In the end, it is only thanks to the children that the Stick's plot to kidnap a child and rob George's house is unsuccessful. In *Five Go Adventuring Again*, the substitute is Mr. Roland, who is

101

hired by the parents to teach the children during their vacation. He is liked by everybody but George and eventually turns out to be a spy who is after the important scientific work of George's father.

Again, the Nancy Drew books are much simpler. The texts do not offer substitutes but rather two options: either you are a criminal or you are a virtuous person who helps to catch criminals. Moreover, the texts hardly allow for any surprises concerning the criminals, and Nancy almost always knows who they are, almost from the beginning, sometimes even before meeting them!

THE CRIMINALS

The preceding discussion has shown that Blyton compensates for the need to portray peaceful relations with parents by increasing the negative attributions of their substitutes. She does this mainly by placing the substitutes into the group of criminals with whom the children fight, a group that stands opposite the parents on the value scale of the text. The criminals as fixtures in every text provide a satisfactory solution for the need to create the opposing worlds of children and adults. They do not violate the ethos of the text, yet they play an important role in the development of the adventure. The criminals are either parent-substitutes or people of inferior social standing (often physically and/or mentally defective and almost always rude and violent). Note the description of Mr. Stick in *Five Run Away Together:* "He was not a very pleasant sight. He had not shaved for some days, and his cheeks and chin were bluish-black . . . his hands were black and so were his finger-nails. He had untidy hair, much too long, and a nose exactly like Edgar's" (42). Moreover, one feature is common to all criminals with no exception—they are ruthless to pets, especially dogs. Cruelty to pets (the children always have a dog—Timmy of the Five, Scamper of the Seven) even becomes a distinguishing sign of criminals because the dog's disapproval of a person foreshadows a later negative evaluation by the text. The scope allotted to a person's attitude toward the children's dog (and vice versa) equals and even exceeds all other characterizations. As a matter of fact, more often than not very little is known about the criminals, but much is always known about their attitude toward the dog. For instance, Mr. Roland's dislike for dogs and Timmy's indifference to him serve as the first clues to suspect him in *Five Go Adventuring Again,* as does Timmy's apparent distaste for Martin and his father in *Five on Kirrin Island Again.* But when the great-grand-father of *Five on Finniston Farm* seems to be ruthless, his genuine good nature is revealed in his attitude toward Timmy:

> George was staring in amazement at Timmy. "He's never done a thing like that before," she said.
> "All dogs are like that with old Granddad." (*Five on Finniston Farm,* 31)

This device helps to emphasize the children's point of view because it adopts their scale of evaluation; the children, as different from adults, judge people this way. In Blyton's books, their judgment is eventually revealed as a just one.

In the Nancy Drew series there is no need for such distinguishing signs as dislike of pets or physical looks because Nancy seldom makes mistakes in identifying the criminals. She usually identifies them promptly, and I have not found a single case where she was mistaken. In one instance, she concludes that it is the postman's stepbrother, just from hearing that the postman indeed has a brother (*Nancy's Mysterious Letter*). In other cases she immediately knows who the criminal is either after seeing his hand or his silhouette:

> She remembered where she had seen a hand like that! It belonged to a fellow who used to work at Larry's service station. She had not liked his insolent manner. (*The Secret of the Wooden Lady,* 16)

> Nancy became excited upon hearing this description of Brex. The footprints in the wood had been those of a tall, slender man! (*The Ghost of Blackwood Hall,* 21)

However, both in the Nancy Drew series and in Blyton's books, the children's efforts to solve the mystery and fight against the criminals are always the core of the story. Their correct judgment and adept instincts in fighting crime are present in every text. In fact, it may well be that the "raison d'être" of the texts' adventure is to reveal the children's virtue and judgment in contrast to those of adults. The latter, while not active participants in the adventure, often become

103

obstacles to the children's successful efforts. Such an obstacle is the policeman Goon (a constant figure in the mysteries of "Fatty" and his friends), who always tries to prevent the children from solving crimes. Invariably he fails to solve the mystery himself; moreover, he is always surprised to find out that the children did manage to follow the right clues and thus to draw the right conclusions (see *The Mystery of Holly Lane* and *The Mystery of Tally-Ho Cottage*).

Still, as soon as the children manage to solve the mystery and the story almost reaches its end, adults who previously disappeared from the scene re-enter it. Reunion of the previously opposing worlds is achieved and the regular hierarchy is back in order, once parents and/or police inspectors take over and criminals are handed to them.

> Peter told his father and mother what had happened and his father, in amazement, went to examine Kerry Blue. . . .
> "Good work!" said the inspector . . . "Very good work indeed." (*The Secret Seven*, 89–90, 93)

> "I certainly think these children deserve a reward for the good work they have done," remarked the inspector. (*Five Run Away Together*, 180)

> "The inspector's awfully pleased with us," said Julian. "And so is Sir James Lawton-Harrison, too, apparently. We're to get a reward." (*Five on a Secret Trail*, 182)

Like the children in Blyton's books, Nancy Drew also manages to solve crimes without the police's help. Nevertheless, she enjoys their appreciation and cooperation, as is seen in *The Secret of the Wooden Lady:* " 'Thanks very much, Miss Drew,' the [police] officer said. 'Just one more debt this department owes you' " (17). Sometimes, however, the police officers envy her efforts (check, for instance, *Nancy's Mysterious Letter*, 24).

In most cases, though, the police do not take part in the mystery itself and come to Nancy's help when everything is almost over and the reunion of the two worlds is achieved; for example, in *The Bungalow Mystery* the police arrive toward the end, just at the right moment to arrest the criminals whom Nancy so skillfully has managed to find: "She was right. Help had come! A moment later police and emergency squad cars stopped at the top of the ravine. Four officers, two stretcherbearers and a doctor, clad in white, hurried down to the group" (169). Until then, until the reunion of the two opposite worlds, the text maintains an exclusive world of children.

THE CREATION OF A CHILDREN'S WORLD

How does Blyton manage to build an exclusive world of children? The creation of a children's world is primarily achieved by separating the two worlds and by focusing on children who solve serious and even dangerous mysteries by themselves. Clearly, the children do take risks and endanger themselves. In *The Secret Seven,* Peter and Jack are caught by the criminals, who subsequently beat them and lock them in the cupboard and later in the cellar. In *Five Go to Smugglers' Top,* the children are caught by the smugglers, who imprison them in the underground tunnels and leave them to starve and suffer; likewise, the kidnappers of *Five Have a Wonderful Time* imprison the children, only this time in the high castle tower. In *Five on Kirrin Island Again,* the children's lives are in danger as the criminals threaten to blow up the whole island.

Nancy Drew also seems to find herself in threatening situations. Usually she gets locked in at least once in every mystery. Often before that, she is either hit or kidnapped, as is evident from the following three examples:

The arm was tight against Nancy's throat; a man's arm in a rough coat sleeve, cutting off her breathing. His fingers pressed into her left shoulder. (*The Secret of the Wooden Lady,* 6)

Nancy told them how the hand had clutched at her throat when the lights went out in the studio.
"I tried to scream and couldn't. I was lifted bodily and carried out of the room."
"Where?" George asked.
"I couldn't see. A cold, wet cloth was clapped over my face. I was taken to the basement of an empty house and left there, bound hand and foot." (*The Ghost of Blackwood Hall,* 36)

Apparently prepared for such emergencies, the two men pulled heavy cords from their pockets and tightly bound the girls.

Karl Driscoll dragged in Susan, who was also tied up, and the three girls were forced roughly down the cellar stairs, through the passage, and into the beach house. Raskin locked the cellar door from the inside and pocketed the key. . . . Karl rasped, "You girls will never see daylight again." (*The Clue of the Broken Locket*, 167–68)

The impression of a children's world is created not only by focusing on the children's adventures and adopting their evaluation; this effect is further enhanced by the creation of an environment of children—in essence by "framing" their world. This framing, in which a temporary boundary between children and adults is erected, becomes possible thanks to three devices (aside from the handling of the adult world): the stylistic level, the location of the adventure and its timing, and the description of the way the children pass their time. All three devices, which will be described here briefly, contribute to the portrayal of a separate world for children.

In manipulating the stylistic level, Blyton not only uses simple vocabulary but also utilizes words whose stylistic function is to designate a child's world. In this connection, her common use of various expressions and exclamations are of special importance. For instance, "bother," "blow," "golly," "gosh," "bags I don't do that," "fibber," "old thing," and "never say die" appear frequently and emphasize the existence of the children's world.

In Nancy Drew books, an even simpler vocabulary and syntax is used; the lexicon of the text is very limited and the syntax tends to cut sentences short. However, I could not trace a similar use of expressions and exclamations, except for George's use of "Hypers." The reason for this could be the girls' age (they are adolescents and not children), or because the series has other devices (which Blyton's lacks) to create the girls' world, such as the descriptions of their looks, dress, and cars. The following detailed description of Nancy's dress, and her careful and skillful driving habits reveal her distinctly adolescent world:

I'll wear my raccoon coat to the game, but I ought to have a hat in the Emerson colors. Orange and violet—hm! Perhaps one of those snappy new sport ones in violet with an orange feather. My lavender evening dress with the—no, I'll wear the deep yellow one with a corsage of violets. (*Nancy's Mysterious Letter*, 81)

Nancy's new car had all the latest devices and its clever driver certainly utilized them, yet without taking undue chances. . . .

The swift autumnal twilight had set in, and Nancy switched on her parking lights to comply with the "sunset law." Although traffic was still thick in the heart of the city, Nancy threaded through it without difficulty. (*Nancy's Mysterious Letter*, 17, 28).

But the most important device that Blyton (and to a certain degree Keene) utilizes in order to frame the children's world is not the stylistic level; the effect of framing the children's world is mostly achieved by descriptions of the times the children spend together. In all of Blyton's books, children spend much of their time eating. Probably assuming that children are attracted to food as adults are to sex, Blyton seldom avoids an opportunity to describe vividly the children's meals, as the following extracts illustrate:

"Fried sausages and onions, potatoes, a tin of sliced peaches and I'll make a custard," said Anne, at once. (*Five Have a Wonderful Time*, 32)

They opened a tin of meat, cut huge slices of bread and made sandwiches. Then they opened a tin of pineapple chunks and ate those, spooning them out of the tin, full of sweetness and juice. After that, they still felt hungry, so they opened two tins of sardines and dug them out with biscuits. It made a really grand meal. (*Five Run Away Together*, 103)

Soon, they were all sitting down at the tea-table, glad to see a wonderful spread! Great slices of thickly buttered bread, home-made jam, home-made cheese, a fat ginger cake, a fruit cake, a dish of ripe plums, and even a home cooked ham if anyone wanted something more substantial. (*Five on Finniston Farm*, 165)

The same phenomenon appears in Nancy Drew books, though in a less prominent manner. Each text devotes at least several paragraphs to a detailed account of Nancy's delicious meals, as the following excerpts describe:

Hannah announced dinner, and the girls went into the dining room. . . . Plates of clear tomato soup with brown crispy croutons were awaiting them. (*Nancy's Mysterious Letter*, 95)

Nancy poured two glasses of milk. Lastly, she made a crisp salad of
lettuce and tomatoes and marinated it with a tangy French dressing.
(*The Bungalow Mystery*, 46)

The dinner was delicious. Bess could not resist topping hers off with
pecan pie. (*The Clue of the Broken Locket*, 8)

The fixation upon the children's meals, besides being a good way to
fill up the pages, is part of Blyton's effort to adopt the children's point
of view; this effort is further seen in her manipulation of time and
location. As previously discussed, Blyton's adventures usually take
place during vacations, when deviations from everyday rules are permitted, even within the strict framework of middle-class values. For
example, the adventures in *The Mystery of Tally-Ho Cottage, Five Go
Adventuring Again, Five on Kirrin Island Again, Five Go Off in a Caravan, Five Go to Smugglers' Top,* and *Five on Finniston Farm* all occur
during vacations. Even when it is not vacation, the children's secret
meetings do not take place in "regular territory." Blyton's consistency
in handling this matter is rather surprising. Not even in a single adventure do the children gather at their own houses (unless a house
becomes extraneous for some reason). Sometimes the children meet
in the shade at the bottom of their garden ("Fatty's" garden or Peter
and Janet's of the Seven); other times, Blyton goes as far as sending
them away—perhaps to the nearest island (*Five on a Treasure Island*)
or even as far as Faynights Castle where they spend their vacations
on gypsy caravans (*Five Have a Wonderful Time*), which become modern caravans in *Five Go to Smugglers' Top.*
    Such consistency cannot be observed in Nancy Drew books, as
some of the mysteries are solved when she is at home (see *The Secret
of the Old Clock* and *Nancy's Mysterious Letter*). Still, her father is usually absent and so her home becomes her own territory. Quite a few
Nancy Drew mysteries, nevertheless, also occur when she is far away
from home (*The Bungalow Mystery, The Mystery of the Fire Dragon, The
Clue of the Broken Locket*). Sometimes Nancy even goes so far as
to fly to Arizona (in *The Secret of Shadow Ranch*) or to leave the
United States for South America (in *The Mystery of the Brass Bound
Trunk*).

By using such techniques, Blyton and Keene manage to achieve the
physical separation of adults and children. The deictic oppositions

are not just a metaphor but create a reality in which two distinct territories exist. It is only toward the end of the story, when the territorial separation disappears and the children have returned to their ordinary territory, that the two opposing worlds merge into one. Once the children are back to everyday life, the ordinary hierarchy governed by middle-class values prevails. The temporary illusion that Blyton and Keene create of an exclusive children's world disappears—only to appear in the next adventure, and attract more and more enthusiastic child readers and less and less adult approval.

Texts

ENID BLYTON'S WORKS

The Mystery:
The Mystery of Holly Lane. 1953. London: Metheun.
The Mystery of Tally-Ho Cottage. 1954. London: Methuen.

The Four:
The Adventurous Four. [1941] 1972. London: Dean and Son.
The Adventurous Four Again [1947] 1973. London: Dean and Son.

The Five:
Five on a Treasure Island. 1942. London: Hodder and Stoughton. 1950. New York: Crowell.
Five Go Adventuring Again. 1943. London: Hodder and Stoughton. 1951. New York: Crowell.
Five Run Away Together. [1944] 1964. London: Hodder and Stoughton.
Five Go to Smugglers' Top. 1945. London: Hodder and Stoughton.
Five Go Off in a Caravan. 1946. London: Hodder and Stoughton.
Five on Kirrin Island Again. 1947. London: Hodder and Stoughton.
Five Have a Wonderful Time. [1952] 1963. London: Hodder and Stoughton.
Five on a Secret Trail. [1956] 1978. London: Hodder and Stoughton.
Five on Finniston Farm. [1960] 1978. London: Hodder and Stoughton.
Five Are Together Again. [1963] 1978. London: Hodder and Stoughton.

The Seven:
The Secret Seven. [1949] 1977. London: Hodder and Stoughton. Published as *The Secret Seven and the Mystery of the Empty House.* 1972. Chicago: Children's Press.

Well Done, Secret Seven. 1951. Leicester: Brockhampton Press. Published as
The Secret Seven and the Tree House Adventure. 1972. Chicago: Children's
Press.
The Secret Seven on the Trail. 1952. Leicester: Brockhampton Press. Published as *The Secret Seven and the Railroad Mystery*. 1972. Chicago: Children's Press.
Secret Seven Fireworks. 1959. Leicester: Brockhampton Press. Published as
The Secret Seven and the Bonfire Mystery. 1972. Chicago: Children's Press.
Shock for the Secret Seven. 1961. Leicester: Brockhampton Press. Published
as *The Secret Seven and the Case of the Dog Lover*. 1972. Chicago: Children's
Press.

THE NANCY DREW SERIES

The Secret of the Old Clock. 1930. New York: Grosset and Dunlop.
Nancy's Mysterious Letter. 1932. New York: Grosset and Dunlop.
The Haunted Shadow Boat. [1937] 1972. London and Glasgow: Collins.
The Mystery of the Brass Bound Trunk. 1940. New York: Grosset and Dunlop.
The Bungalow Mystery. [1940] 1960. New York: Grosset and Dunlop.
The Secret of Shadow Ranch. [1945] 1971. London and Glasgow: Collins.
The Ghost of Blackwood Hall. [1947] 1975. London: Fontana Paperbacks.
The Mystery of the Fire Dragon. 1961. New York: Grosset and Dunlop.
The Clue of the Broken Locket. 1965. New York: Grosset and Dunlop.
The Secret of the Wooden Lady. 1967. New York: Grosset and Dunlop.

Chapter Five

Translation
of Children's Literature

 This chapter covers certain behavior patterns of children's literature. The discussion is based mainly on research into translations of children's books into Hebrew, though the described patterns of behavior are not necessarily typical only to Hebrew children's literature, but seem to be common to other national systems as well (mainly to dependent systems such as the Icelandic, the Arabic, the Swedish; see Klingberg, Ørvig, and Stuart 1978 and Even-Zohar 1978a). The act of translation is understood here not in the traditional normative sense, but rather as a semiotic concept. Thus, translation is understood as part of a transfer mechanism—that is, the process by which textual models of one system are transferred to another. In this process, certain products are produced within the target system, which relate in various and complex ways to products of the source system. Hence, the final product of the act of translation is the result of the relationship between a source system and a target system, a relationship that is itself determined by a certain hierarchy of semiotic constraints (see Jakobson 1959, Toury 1980a, Even-Zohar 1981). The texts that will be analyzed here do not include only what has been traditionally discussed as translated texts, but abridgments and adaptations as well. The primary condition for their inclusion in this study is that they claim some sort of relationship between themselves and the original.

In viewing translation as part of a transfer process, it must be stressed that the subject at stake is not just translations of texts from one language to another, but also the translations of texts from one system to another—for example, translations from the adult system

111

into the children's. Since the point of departure for this discussion is the understanding of children's literature not as an assemblage of elements existing in a vacuum but as an integral part of the literary polysystem, the transfer from one system to another is even more crucial for my discussion. Hence, I wish to examine the implications of the systemic status of children's literature to substantiate the claim that the behavior of translation of children's literature is largely determined by the position of children's literature within the literary polysystem.

Translated children's literature was chosen for discussion because it is believed to be a convenient methodological tool for studying norms of writing for children. In fact, the discussion of translated texts is even more fruitful than that of original texts because translational norms expose more clearly the constraints imposed on a text that enters the children's system. This is true because in transferring the text from the source into the target system translators are forced to take into account systemic constraints. I contend that this holds especially true for texts transferred from adult to children's literature, texts whose status in the literary polysystem has changed historically. This group of texts (such as *Robinson Crusoe* and *Gulliver's Travels*), considered classics for children, will be analyzed as a sample for discussion of two issues: the norms of translating children's books (as opposed to those of adult literature) and the systemic constraints determining those norms.

Norms of Translating Children's Books

Unlike contemporary translators of adult books, the translator of children's literature can permit himself great liberties regarding the text, as a result of the peripheral position of children's literature within the literary polysystem.[1] That is, the translator is permitted to manipulate the text in various ways by changing, enlarging, or abridging it or by deleting or adding to it. Nevertheless, all these

---

[1] Those liberties were once the prevalent norm in translation of adult books. But long after they had ceased to exist in adult literature, they were and still are acceptable, if not prevalent, in the children's system, not only because of its self-perpetuating nature, but also because of its image in society.

translational procedures are permitted only if conditioned by the translator's adherence to the following two principles on which translation for children is based: an adjustment of the text to make it appropriate and useful to the child, in accordance with what society regards (at a certain point in time) as educationally "good for the child"; and an adjustment of plot, characterization, and language to prevailing society's perceptions of the child's ability to read and comprehend.

These two principles, rooted in the self-image of children's literature, have had different hierarchal relations in different periods. Thus, for instance, as long as the concept of didactic children's literature prevailed, the first principle, based on the understanding of children's literature as a tool for education, was dominant. Nowadays, the emphasis differs; although to a certain degree the first principle still dictates the character of the translations, the second principle, that of adjusting the text to the child's level of comprehension, is more dominant. Yet it is possible that the two principles might not always be complementary: sometimes they might even contradict each other. For example, it might be assumed that a child is able to understand a text involved with death, and yet at the same time the text may be regarded as harmful to his mental welfare. In such a situation, the translated text might totally delete one aspect in favor of another, or perhaps even include contradictory features, because the translator hesitated between the two principles. In any case, these usually complementary principles determine each stage of the translation process. They dictate decisions concerned with the textual selection procedure (which texts will be chosen for translation), as well as with permissible manipulation. They also serve as the basis for the systemic affiliation of the text. But most important of all, in order to be accepted as a translated text for children, to be affiliated with the children's system, the final translated product must adhere to these two principles, or at least not violate them.

The Systemic Affiliation

The systemic affiliation of a text entering the children's system is very similar to that of a text entering another peripheral system—the non-canonized system for adults. As noted in my discussion of the self-image of children's literature in chapter 2, historically both systems use models prominent in the early stages of the canonized adult system. I have also noted that the models of both are frequently secondary models transformed from adult literature. For instance, in ambivalent texts the model of the fairy tale became acceptable in English children's literature only after the Romantic school had introduced and developed imagination and rejected realism—although realism did continue to prevail in children's literature. Gradually imagination became acceptable in children's literature (mainly through translation of folktales and artistic fairies, such as Andersen's) until finally it became the prevailing norm.

Yet, it should be noted that in children's literature, the model transferred from adult literature does not function as a secondary model. Within the framework of children's literature, it functions initially as a primary model. Later it might be transformed into the non-canonized children's literature, usually in a simplified and reduced form. The detective story in children's literature might illustrate this point. The model was transferred to children's literature only after it had been canonized by adult literature (mainly through Dostoyevsky's *Crime and Punishment* and Doyle's *Sherlock Holmes*). It was first accepted by the canonized children's literature system where it functioned as a primary model, different in character from that of the adult model (see Erich Kästner's *Emil und die Detektive* [1928] and R. J. McGregor's *The Young Detectives* [1934]). Only after it had been accepted and legitimized by the canonized children's system was the detective story transferred into non-canonized children's literature, though in a reduced and simplified form. Here it served as the basis for one of the most prominent models of children's literature over the last fifty years. Every Western children's literature has its own popular detective series, whether it be the American Nancy Drew and Hardy Boys or the English series of Enid Blyton.

However, despite the great similarity between non-canonized adult literature and children's literature regarding their systemic affiliation, a big difference remains between them. As mentioned earlier, the primary difference lies in the fact that the children's system by itself is stratified into two main subsystems—canonized and non-canonized; an even more fundamental difference lies in the different source of constraints imposed on the text as a result of its affiliation. Though the constraints themselves may be similar (as in the case with the nonacceptability of primary models), their motivation and legitimation differ altogether. Whereas in the case of the non-canonized adult system the main constraint is commercial, the source of constraints in the canonized children's system is mainly educational.

These systemic constraints of the children's system are perhaps best manifested in the following aspects: the affiliation of the text to existing models; the integrality of the text's primary and secondary models, the degree of complexity and sophistication of the text; the adjustment of the text to ideological and didactic purposes; and the style of the text.

Affiliation to Existing Models

Translation of children's literature tends to relate the text to existing models in the target system. This phenomenon, known from general translational procedures (see Even-Zohar 1975, 1978d, Toury 1977, 1980a, 1980b), is particularly prominent in the translation of children's literature because of the system's tendency to accept only the conventional and the well known. If the model of the original text does not exist in the target system, the text is changed by deleting or by adding such elements as will adjust it to the integrating model of the target system. This phenomenon also existed in the past in various adult literatures, although long after it ceased to be prevalent in the adult canonized system, it still remained prominent in children's literature.

Test Cases: *Gulliver's Travels* and *Robinson Crusoe*

The various adaptations and translations of *Gulliver's Travels* will serve as a good example. The abridged version of *Gulliver's Travels* was read by children in the form of a chapbook soon after it was originally issued in 1726. As with another successful novel, *Robinson Crusoe*, *Gulliver's Travels* was quickly reissued in an unauthorized abridged version (and as a chapbook) soon after publishers realized its commercial potential. With *Robinson Crusoe* the first part was published in April 1719, and already in August of that same year an abridged and unauthorized version of the text was published, followed by dozens of chapbook editions during the eighteenth century.[2] The same was true of *Gulliver's Travels* (1726), whose first abridged and unauthorized versions were published by 1727 and contained only "Lilliput" and "Brobdingnag." By the middle of the eighteenth century, quite a few editions of *Gulliver's Travels* were published in the form of chapbooks, containing only "Lilliput." Both abridged versions of *Robinson Crusoe* and *Gulliver's Travels* continued to appear even at the beginning of the nineteenth century, but by that time they were issued for children and young people only (see Perrin 1969).

Originally, the lack of any other appealing reading material was the main reason for *Gulliver's Travels* being adopted by the children's system. Like all chapbooks, the book was enthusiastically read by children, in the absence of other literature written specifically for them (see chapter 6), and in such a way filled a gap that still existed in the literary polysystem. Thus, the text was read by children even before the children's system actually existed; since then, over the last two centuries it has managed to occupy a prominent position in the children's system.[3] This is the case not only because it quickly became a "classic" for children, but mainly because *Gulliver's Travels* was continuously revised and adapted, in order to be affiliated with the target system.

---

[2] When model affiliation is dealt with historically, Defoe's *Robinson Crusoe* is even more interesting and complicated. Very briefly, this is the pattern: The original *Robinson Crusoe* served as a model for the *Robinsonnades* that became prominent in the children's literature and were a reduced and simplified model of the original *Robinson Crusoe*. Translators who later adjusted *Robinson Crusoe* to children's literature could therefore ignore the original model and transformed the *Robinsonnade*, into a prominent model of children's literature.

[3] As the abridged text became a classic for children in the nineteenth century, it simultaneously lost its position in the adult system. This does not mean that the text disappeared altogether from the adult system. On the contrary, the text acquired the status of a "canon," as part of the literary heritage; that is, the text is read today by adults on the basis of its historical value, while in children's literature it is still read as a "living" text.

What were the implications of the process by which the text was affiliated to the children's system? The first decision that translators had to make concerned the very selection of the text. This decision was in a way incidental because the text that already existed as a chapbook became later on a chapbook for children. However, what was common to the chapbooks and all other adaptations of *Gulliver's Travels* was their inclusion of only the first two books. In spite of the fact that *Gulliver's Travels* was frequently translated, not a single translation for children has included all four books. Most translations are of the first book only, and several others include the second book as well. The selection of the first two books is primarily connected with the decision to transfer the text from its original form as a satire into a fantasy or adventure story.

At first the text was transferred either into the model of fantasy or adventure just because they were such popular models in chapbooks. Later on, the same decision was the result of two additional factors: first, the overwhelming popularity of fantasy and adventure in children's literature as well; and second, the lack of satire as a genre in the target system (children's literature totally ignored the existence of such a genre). This was probably due to the fact that children were not supposed to be either acquainted with the subjects of the satire, nor with its meaning. Translators who wished to transform the text from a satire into either model (fantasy or adventure) of the target system had to omit the last two books for two reasons. Satire is built into *Gulliver's Travels* in sophisticated and complex ways, including the inter-relations of the four books. In wishing to avoid the satire, translators had no further interest in retaining that now functionless relationship and could thus easily forego the other books entirely. Next, translators found it much easier to adjust elements of the first two books into models of the target system. For instance, the people of Lilliput could much more easily be transformed into dwarfs of a fantasy story than the people of the Country of Houyhnhnms, for whom it was almost impossible to find an equivalent in the models that already existed in the target system. Moreover, Gulliver's travels in unknown countries, as well as his battles and wars, could easily serve as the basis for an adventure story. However, when a translator decides upon one of the models, usually in accordance with the presumed age of the reader—fantasy for younger children, adventure story for older—the other model usually creeps into the text and thus both models can be discerned almost in all translations.

Those two models, contradictory by nature (fantasy tending to generalization, while the adventure story tends to concretization), dictate the very selection of the text and its manipulation. The transformation of the Lilliputian people into the dwarfs of the fantasy story exemplifies the model's manipulation of the text. While the original text emphasizes the similarity between the people of Lilliput and the people of Gulliver's country (who differ mainly in size but resemble each other in other respects—which then becomes the core of the satire), translators deliberately make every effort to blur the similarity and create an opposition that does not exist in the original, that is, an opposition between two worlds—the world of Gulliver and the fantasy world of the dwarfs. The fantasy world of the dwarfs has all the typical attributes of the model of the fantasy, especially as far as the fabula and characterization are concerned. Hence, in the adaptation for children, the dwarfs are part of an enchanted and strange world full of glory and magnificence. They are innocent little creatures forced to protect themselves against a negative force that has appeared in their world—a typical fabula of fairy tales. In such a way the Lilliputians are no more an object of criticism and satire but an object of identification and pity.

The opposition between Gulliver's original world and that of the Lilliputians is further revealed in adaptations for children by the description of both the emperor and his people in terms of the fantasy model. Thus, the creatures of the original text become "*strange* creatures" (p. 9), the inhabitants become "*dwarfs* inhabiting the country" (p. 9), and "four of the inhabitants" become "four men of the native *dwarfs*" (Jizreel edition, my italics).[4]

Moreover, unlike the original text, which uses several devices to emphasize the difference in size in order to hint at potential resemblance in other respects, translations alway present the Lilliputians not as miniature human beings but as dwarfs, as creatures *different* from human beings. As a result, they emphasize their size by adding diminutive epithets. In the original text the description of the arrows compares the Lilliputians to needles: "I felt above a hundred

---

[4] All English translations of the Hebrew *Gulliver's Travels* are mine.

arrows discharged on my left hand, which prickled me like so many needles" (p. 18). The translations add to the description of the arrows the diminutive epithet "tiny and minute" (Massada version). In the same way translations add "tiny as a fly" to the food Gulliver eats (Massada version), which is originally described as: "shoulders, legs and loins shaped like those of mutton, and very well dressed, but smaller than the wings of a lark" (19). Furthermore, devices that are used by the original text to create the sense of the size of the Lilliputian world, such as accurate and detailed numbers, situations which create the sense of proportion (the children playing in his hair), are totally omitted because their original function was to emphasize the similarity between the two worlds, described originally as different only in size.

The same phenomenon of adaptation of the original text into the models of the target system can also be discerned in the characterization of the Lilliputians. Thus, while the original text presents complicated characterization of both Gulliver and the Lilliputians, translators tend to offer unequivocal presentations and hence to maintain the typical opposition between "good" and "bad" of both the fantasy and the adventure models. As a result, whereas in the original, the "good" features of Lilliputians are only part of their characterization and are accompanied by harsh criticism, translators tend to include only the "good" features, thus changing the characterization altogether. For instance, the criticism of the strange relations between parents and children and the absurd manners of burial of the original are totally omitted in translations, while good manners and high morality are indeed retained. An even more interesting example is the device for the manipulation of the threatening or tension-producing element, required for the model of the target system. Once a certain character is chosen to represent this element, the translation will ignore all other components, save the negative feature of the character, such as his mischievous use of power (see the description of the Chief Admiral in the El Hamaayan edition, 41; or in the Jizreel edition, 35).

This attempt to adjust the description of the Lilliputian world to the model of fantasy can be observed in the description of the emperor as well. In the original, the emperor's description is detailed and based on many aspects—his height, color, voice, body, gestures:

"He is taller, by almost the breadth of my nail than any of his court, which alone is enough to strike an awe into the beholders. His features are strong and masculine, with an Austrian lip and arched nose, his complexion olive, his countenance erect, his body and limbs well proportioned, all his motions graceful, and his deportment majestic" (24). Translators tend to subordinate this type of description to that typical of the fantasy model—to emphasize only his height and impressive appearance as a metonym for his power, and omit all other features. Hence the original description is translated into: "He was a handsome little man much taller than the rest of his court" (Ladybird, 17) or "All his subjects dreaded his height" (Jizreel, 19). In such a way translators changed the original description of the emperor, which was based on popular travel books of the time, and transferred them to the stereotyped presentation common to fairy tales, in which descriptions of kings and rulers are aimed mainly at emphasizing the element of power.

The same phenomenon can be discerned in the description of the emperor's dress and sword. In the original text the description of the emperor's dress is as follows:

> I have had him since many times in my hand, and therefore cannot be deceived in the description. His dress was very plain and simple, and the fashion of it between the Asiatic and the European; but he had on his head a light helmet of gold, adorned with jewels, and a plume on the crest. He held his sword drawn in his hand, to defend himself, if I should happen to break loose; it was almost three inches long, the hilt and scabbard were gold enriched with diamonds. (24)

Various translators have omitted most of this detailed description, leaving only that which is typical of fairy-tale emperors—glory and wealth—and frequently using the sword to symbolize the emperor's power: "In his hand the King held his drawn sword whose handle was decorated with sparkling diamonds" (El Hamaayan, 16); "He held in his hand a sceptre bigger than a match. Its handle and edges were decorated with jewels" (Massada, 26); and "In his hand the Emperor held his drawn sword, a little shorter than a knitting needle. Its golden handle and scabbard sparkled with diamonds" (Zelkowitz, 21). It should be noted, however, that the process of adjusting the text to a certain model involves more than mere omissions of certain elements. One of the most interesting manifestations of text adjustment are those elements that translators find necessary to add to the original. These added elements are the best indicators of the force of constraints on the model, since adding new elements to an already shortened text implies that the translator regards them as indispensable to the model. Additions are thus needed to reinforce the model, and their inclusion reveals even more than deletions do which elements are considered obligatory for the target model. As an example of such an addition, note that the "plain and simple" dress of the original became in the translation "magnificent and very special" (Sinai 23). Another example of added elements to the text is that in which the original text describes the man who speaks with Gulliver as "a person of quality." The translator made him a typical character of the fantasy model, "a man wearing a long and expensive cloak and a little boy holding it behind" (Sreberk).

In summary, the model's affiliation determined which texts would be included or excluded, which elements would be added or omitted, and which would remain, albeit with changed functions. In the translations for children, the satirical elements have either entirely vanished or remained minus their original function, usually acquiring a new function and in this way contributing to the model of the target system. In some cases they have even remained without any function at all. Thus, by leaving out some elements and by changing the functions of others, translators have managed to adjust the text to prevalent models of the target system.

The Text's Integrality

Today the norm of a complete, unabridged text is accepted in most translations of the adult canonized system. Deletions, if at all, are incidental. But in the nineteenth century and even at the beginning of the twentieth, such a norm was not obligatory, and translators were allowed to manipulate the integrality of the original text (see Toury 1977). In the adult system, this freedom to manipulate exists only in the noncanonized system. Here translators are free to add or delete in accordance with the demands of the target system, and more often than not they do not preserve the completeness of the original text (see, for instance, Hebrew translations of James Bond).

The same freedom of manipulation seems to exist in the children's system (even within the body of canonized literature) particularly when adult books are transferred into it. Within this body, the "raison d'être" for all abridged texts for children is based on the supposition that children are incapable of reading lengthy texts. Nevertheless, the actual decision of what to omit is the result of the need to revise the text in accordance with two main criteria, in addition to the systemic affiliation: first, the norms of morality accepted and demanded by the children's system; second, the assumed level of the child's comprehension. Hence a translator's decision to adjust the text to children invariably means that he will have to shorten it and make it less complicated at the same time. These two procedures might, in reality, contradict one another because fewer elements are required to carry more functions. As a result, translators must carefully manipulate the text in order to maintain a workable balance, always keeping those two principles in focus.

The simplest manipulation of the text is done by deleting undesirable elements or whole paragraphs. However, this option is not always available to the translator. Sometimes the need to delete certain scenes turns out to be very problematical for the translator, especially when they are regarded as indispensable for the development of the plot. Such scenes are often altered to become suitable when the translator finds an acceptable formula or format for their inclusion. As an example, note the scene of Gulliver saving the palace from the fire by urinating on it. In the original text, the scene of extinguishing the fire is used to advance the plot as well as to integrate satire into the story. The Lilliputians reveal their ingratitude by not thanking Gulliver for saving the palace. On the contrary, they blame him for breaking the law of the kingdom and later use it as an excuse for sending him away. The whole scene is clearly used in order to satirize the arbitrariness of the laws and the ingratitude of the people. However, most translations could neither cope with Gulliver extinguishing the fire by urinating on it (an unacceptable scenario in a children's book) nor with the satire of the kingdom and its laws. On the other hand, some translations, especially those built on the adventure model, did not wish to leave out such a dramatic episode. In these versions, Gulliver does extinguish the fire either by throwing water on it (Mizrachi) or by blowing it out (Zelkovitz). As a result, this episode is left in the text, even though it contradicts the entire characterization of Lilliputians as good and grateful people. Here it may be observed that in order to maintain the integrality of the plot, which is clearly the most important aspect in the adventure model (see discussion further on), translators do not hesitate to contradict other components of the text such as characterization. Other translators, however, were happy to delete the entire scene, primarily because it constitutes a violation of the taboo in children's literature on excretions; moreover, it also violates the characterization of the dwarfs as victims. Another reason for its deletion in some translations is that it takes part in the buildup of the satire which translators so religiously try to avoid. Hence, the deletion of this unnecessary scene can be easily justified.

In fact, it can even be formulated as a rule that when it is possible to delete undesirable scenes without damaging the basic plot or characterizations, translators will not hesitate to do so. Hence all translators of *Gulliver's Travels* happily give up the scene where Gulliver is suspected of having a love affair with the queen, for such a scene violates the taboo on sexual activity in children's literature. In the adult version, this scene plays an important role in the satire because it appears logistically impossible for the suspected lovers to have an affair due to their vastly different dimensions. Seen as satire, this incident disappears altogether from translations for children; it is unnecessary and thus can be easily omitted.

The other major criterion that guides translators is their sensitivity to the level of reading comprehension of children. When a translator assumes that a certain paragraph will not be understood by the child, he will either make changes or deletions to adjust it to the "appropriate" comprehenion level. This is why, translators of *Robinson Crusoe* delete the opening dialogue between Robinson and his father, in which the father presents the ethos of the bourgeoisie as opposed to that of the lower and upper classes.

The same phenomenon is also apparent in most translations of *Tom Sawyer*. In the original text, the familiar fence-whitewashing scene has two parts. The first describes Tom's ingenious device for making the children work for him and also pay for that pleasure. In the second, Twain throws out several sarcastic remarks about the "sacred" values of work and pleasure, aiming his irony not toward Tom and his treasures, but rather toward adults, whose values the text compares to those of the children. The result is a mocking and condescending attitude vis-à-vis adults. Most translators delete this part of the scene entirely, and thus the ironical level of the scene is completely expunged (Twain 1911, 1940, 1960). There are quite a few reasons for this deletion. First, this passage does not contribute directly to the "plot" in its narrowest sense. Translators, in spite of their endeavors to make longer texts shorter, are reluctant to omit a paragraph that has a substantive part in the "plot." This is because action and plot are considered the most important elements of children's books or in Nina Bawden's words: "Writing for children is not easier than writing for adults; it is different. The *story-line,* clearly, has to be stronger. . . . The clue to what they really enjoy is what they reread, what they go back to, and this is almost always a book with a strong *narrative line*" (Bawden 1974, 6, my italics). However, in a paragraph considered nonessential to the plot, translators will happily exclude it. In addition, many translators feel uneasy in presenting ironical attitudes toward life and toward grown-ups that do not suit the values a child should be acquiring through literature. They justify their omission of irony by suggesting that such sophisticated attitudes, which demand a two-dimensional confrontation, cannot be understood by the child. Hence, whenever it is possible, the level of irony is totally excluded so as to make the text less complicated.

This tendency to avoid complex and/or unflattering characterizations of adults, and especially of parents, can be seen in other cases as well. As Wunderlich and Morrissey argue in their analysis of translations of *Pinocchio,* Geppetto's description is subject to the same procedure:

> Geppetto, the image of the parent, also undergoes change. The original Geppetto is a truly human figure. He displays anger, rage and frustration. . . . The parent loves, but the parent also becomes angry and punishing. Raising a child, Collodi shows, is no easy matter.
>
> Parents, however, are no longer punishing. They display only love, warmth, support, and self-sacrifice towards the child. So, as with Pinocchio, Geppetto is weakened through the thirties; his punishing visage is eroded. (Wunderlich and Morrissey, 1982, 110)

The Level of Complexity of the Text

As stated earlier, the text's integrality is directly affected by the need to shorten the text and the demand for a less complicated text. When shortening a text, translators have to make sure that they also reduce the proportions between elements and functions and make less elements carry even fewer functions. In contrast to adult canonized literature, in which the norm of complexity is the most prevalent today, the norm of simple and simplified models is still prominent in most children's literature (canonized and non-canonized), as is also the case with the non-canonized adult system. This norm, rooted in the self-image of children's literature, tends to determine not only the thematics and characterization of the text, but also its options concerning permissible structures.

When dealing with the question of complexity, the text of *Alice in Wonderland* is most interesting. In chapter 3, I asked how the text came to be accepted by adults and discovered that it was the result of the very characteristics later considered by adaptors and translators as unsuitable for children. Here I approach the problem briefly from the opposite direction—that is, to show how the text became acceptable for children, I ask which textual elements were changed in order to make the text, in the translator's opinion, acceptable for children. As a rule, all the elements that were considered too sophisticated were either changed or deleted. Hence, translators systematically deleted all the satire and parody of the original text. The paragraphs that contained those elements were not at all difficult to omit, because they did not contribute to the plot. Unlike them, the complicated presentation of the world in the text posed a more serious problem for the translators because they could not give it up altogether.

In the original *Alice in Wonderland,* Carroll intentionally made it impossible to determine whether things happen in a dream or in reality. Such a complicated presentation was not acceptable to the translators, who eventually solved the problem by motivating the whole story as a dream. Therefore, the transfer into children's literature resulted in a simplified presentation that insisted on a clear distinction between reality and fantasy. For instance, one adaptation opens in the following way: "Once upon a time there was a little girl called Alice, *who had a very curious dream*" (Modern Promotions, my italics). Another adaptation ends in a phrase which leaves no doubt that it was anything but a dream: " 'I am glad to be back where things are really what they seem,' said Alice, as she woke up from her strange Wonderful dream" (Disney). The procedure of transformation of a text into a less sophisticated one and its adjustment to a simplified model is always achieved either by deletions or by changing the relation between elements and functions. However, it may even happen that some elements will remain in the text, although they lose their original function without acquiring a new one. This occurs because the translator retains certain elements, assuming that they contribute to some level when they actually do not. For example, in the original *Tom Sawyer*, the aunt is ironically described by the funny way she uses her spectacles: "The old lady pulled her spectacles down and looked over them about the room; then she put them up and looked out under them. She seldom or never looked *through* them for so small a thing as a boy; they were her state pair, the pride of her heart, and were built for 'style' not service—she could have seen through a piece of stove lids just as well" (Twain 1935, 287). The comment explains ironically why the aunt puts her spectacles up and down and does not look through them. In one of the translations (Ben-Pinhas 1960), the translator made her lift her spectacles up and down, but left out the writer's comment. The translator probably thought the spectacles contributed to the plot (because of the "action") and did not pay attention to their function in the characterization of the old lady. Hence the spectacles in the translation remained functionless.

Ideological or Evaluative Adaptation

In earlier stages of adult literature, the concept of literature as a didactic instrument for unequivocal values or for a certain ideology was prominent. Long after it ceased to exist in adult literature, this concept was still so powerful in children's literature that translators were ready to completely change the source text in order to have the revised version serve ideological purposes. A typical example for such ideological revision is the translations of *Robinson Crusoe*. Perhaps the most prominent of these was the translation into the German by Joachim Campe (1746–1818) titled *Robinson der Jüngere* (1779–80), which served as a catalyst for further translations: Campe's adaptation was translated by himself into French and English (1781), although the most popular English translation was that of Stockdale, published in 1782 in four volumes. The text was further translated, and by 1800 translations also appeared in Dutch, Italian, Danish, Croatian, Czech, and Latin. Moreover, the text was translated into Hebrew no less than three times (1824, 1849, 1896?, see chapter 7) and even into Yiddish (1784, 1840).

In such a way, *Robinson Crusoe* managed to be preserved in the canonized children's literature for over a century, probably due to its ideological adjustment. Furthermore, the text was followed by various imitations that created one of the most prominent models in children's literature, that of the *Robinsonnade*. Yet, it should be emphasized that although Campe's adaptation was the main reason for *Robinson Crusoe*'s becoming a classic for children, he practically made it into a totally different text, from the ideological point of view, retaining only some of the original setting.

Campe's motivations for translating *Robinson Crusoe* were primarily aimed at adapting it to Rousseau's pedagogical system, which served as the pedagogical system of his school in Dessau. Campe decided to translate *Robinson Crusoe*, because Rousseau himself suggested that it be the only book given to a child due to its portrayal of the individual's struggle with nature. When the book was examined with Rousseau's views in mind, however, it became clear to Campe that it demanded a thorough change—Defoe's views on the bourgeois ethos and colonialist values contradicted those of Rousseau. Thus, in the original text, *Robinson Crusoe* arrives at the island with all the symbols of Western culture (weapons, food, the Bible) and manages to cultivate nature. In Campe's translation, however, he reaches the island naked and possessionless (he even has to spark the fire by rubbing stones). Robinson has to learn to live within nature without building a quasi-European culture. Rather, he builds an anti-European culture and suggests it as an alternative to the European.

When Campe's adaptation was translated into Hebrew (on Campe's status in Hebrew children's literature, see chapter 7), the Hebrew translation needed further ideological revision in order to be adapted to the prevailing Enlightenment views of the nineteenth century. In one of the translations, that of Zamoshch, the translator tried in a rather paradoxical manner to combine Campe's antirationalist views with the views of the Jewish Enlightenment; the latter, in fact, were similar to Defoe's ethos, the belief that a rationalist can overcome nature and even cultivate it. The translator tried to stress not only Rousseauian values, but also those of the Jewish Enlightenment movement such as productivization. Thus, the children listening to the story told by their father do not sit idle, but willingly busy themselves with some sort of work. In this example, it can be seen how a text is selected for adaptation on the basis of ideology, yet still requires ideological revision; paradoxically, the new version resulting from this revision included elements of both Defoe and Campe.

The Stylistic Norms

Discussion in English of the stylistic norms governing translation of children's books into Hebrew is impossible; thus only the guiding principle will be presented here. The prominent stylistic norm in translation into Hebrew of both adult and children's literature is the preference for high literary style whenever possible. Despite the fact that both systems share a common stylistic norm, however, its motivation and legitimation is different in each system. While in adult literature high style is connected with the idea of "literariness" per se, in children's literature it is connected with a didactic concept and the attempt to enrich the child's vocabulary. Again, as long as this didactic concept of children's literature prevails, as long as it is assumed that "books can and do influence outlook, belief and conduct," and that "for this reason, the writer for children will weigh his words carefully" (Collinson 1973, 37–38), then children's literature will not be able to liberate itself either from its diadactic aims or from this specific norm of high style. Even if "literariness" disappears from adult literature, it will still dominate children's literature, as long as it is regarded as educationally "good" and until the didactic concept of children's literature declines or at least loses its sway.

This phenomenon reflects the strong grip that systematic constraints hold on the children's system. These constraints govern not only the selection of texts to be translated from the adult canonized system, but the presentation, characterization, and model affiliation as well.

Texts

ENGLISH EDITIONS

Carroll, Lewis. [1865] 1968. *Alice's Adventures in Wonderland*. New York: MacMillan.
————. [1890] 1966. *The Nursery Alice*. New York: Dover.
Defoe, Daniel. [1719] 1965. *Robinson Crusoe*. Harmondsworth: Penguin.
Swift, Jonathan. [1726] 1960. *Gulliver's Travels*. Cambridge, Mass.: Riverside.
Twain, Mark. [1876] 1935. *The Adventures of Tom Sawyer*. New York: Garden City.

TRANSLATIONS AND ADAPTATIONS

Lewis Carroll:
Carroll, Lewis. 1945. *Alisa be'eretz ha-plaot*. Translated by Avraham Aryeh Akavya. Tel Aviv: Sreberk.
————. 1973. *Alisa be'eretz ha-plaot*. Translated by Bela Bar'am. Tel Aviv: Massada.
Disney, Walt. 1976. *Alisa be'eretz ha-plaot*. Translated by Shulamit Lapid. Tel Aviv: Yavneh.
————. 1980. *Alice in Wonderland*. Racine, Wis.: Golden Press.
Alice's Adventures in Wonderland. Abridged by A. K. Herring. New York: Modern Promotions.

Daniel Defoe:
Campe, Joachim. 1824: *Robinson der Yingere: Eyn Lezebukh fir Kinder*. Eine Hebreische ibertragen fon David Zamoshch. Breslau: Sulzbach.
Robinson Crusoe. 1936. Translated and abridged by Yehuda Grazovski. Tel Aviv: Massada.
Defoe, Daniel. 1964. *Robinson Crusoe*. Translated and abridged by Ben-Pinhas. Tel Aviv: Niv.

Jonathan Swift:
Swift, Jonathan. 1961. *Mas'ei Gulliver*. Translated and adapted by Yaacov Niv. Ramat Gan: Massada.

Gulliver be-artzot haplaot. 1976. Translated by Avraham Aryeh Akavya. Tel Aviv: Jizreel.
Gulliver be-eretz ha-anaqim. Tel Aviv: Zelkowitz.
Massa Lilliput. Translated by Pesah Ginzburg. Tel Aviv: Sreberk.
Gulliver's Travels. Loughborough: Ladybird.

Mark Twain:
Twain, Mark, 1911. *Meoraot Tom.* Translated by Israel Haim Tavyov. Odessa: Turgeman.
Twain, Mark. 1940. *Tom Sawyer.* Translated and abridged by Avraham Aryeh Akavya. Tel Aviv: Jizreel.
Twain, Mark. 1960. *Meoraot Tom Sawyer.* Translated and abridged by Ben-Pinhas. Tel Aviv: Yesod.

Part Three

SYSTEM
AND
HISTORY

Chapter Six

The Model of Development
of Canonized Children's Literature

 The canonized system of books for children began to develop almost a century after a stratified system of adult literature already existed. This is true, of course, if children's literature is discussed as a steady and continuous flow and not as a sporadic activity, like the few children's books published in the sixteenth and seventeenth centuries. Children's literature became a culturally recognized field only in the eighteenth century, and a prominent field within the publishing establishment only from the middle of that same century. The relatively late emergence of children's literature as a systemic form is a complex issue and involves many factors. Thus, in this part of my book on "system and history," I limit my discussion on the origins of children's literature to two major questions: What is the foundation of children's literature? How can we account for its stratification?

Histories of children's literature have paid much attention to the development of children's books in the Western world (especially in the Anglo-Saxon world, but in Germany, France, and Italy as well); abundant material can be found in works such as Darton (1958), Hürlimann (1967), Meigs et al. (1969), Ofek (1979), Thwaite (1972), and others. There is no point in surveying the data described again. Rather, I present them in a structural series and not simply in chronological order, claiming that the same historical model is common to all beginnings of children's literatures. I contend that the very same stages of development reappear in all children's literatures, regardless of when and where they began to develop. That is to say, the historical patterns in the development of children's literature are basically the same in any literature, transcending national and even

133

time boundaries. It does not matter whether two national systems began to develop at the same time, or if one developed a hundred or even two hundred years later (as with Hebrew, and later with Arabic and Japanese children's literatures). They all seem to pass through the very same stages of development without exception. Moreover, the same cultural factors and institutions are involved in their creation.

From the instances of the Puritans in England and America, or the followers of the Jewish Enlightenment in Germany 150 years later, it may be concluded that their ideology formed the basis of canonized children's literature. They all shared the view that in the process of their education, children needed books, and that those books must differ from adult books principally through their fundamental attachment to the educational system itself.

Thus, it was through the framework of the educational system that a canonized children's system began to develop; at the same time, it was the need to combat popular literature from which the stratification of the whole literary system emerged. To deal with these two mutually dependent issues—the function of the educational system in the development of canonized system and the function of chapbooks in the stratification of the system—methodological separation is required. It is more convenient to treat each issue separately in order to highlight the distinct historical factors involved in each; hence, canonized children's literature will be discussed here not only as part of the literary system, but as part of the educational system as well. In the next chapter, the stratification of the children's system and the creation of two new opposing systems—adults versus children and canonized versus non-canonized children's literature—will be dealt with, pointing to the function of chapbooks in this process.

The State of the System Prior to the Eighteenth Century

It cannot be denied that few children's books had been published during the sixteenth and seventeenth centuries (compared to the thousands of books published during the eighteenth and nineteenth centuries and sold in millions), as indicated by Sloane (1955), Welch (1972), Watson (1971), and others. But clearly, children's literature was not yet recognized as a distinct field of culture. Books published prior to the end of the seventeenth century were composed mainly of "courtesy books," such as the English translation of Erasmus's *A Lytelle Booke of Good Manners for Chyldren* (1532) or Francis Seager's *The School of Vertue and Booke of Good Nourture for Chyldren to Learn Theyr Dutie By* (1557), which can only be regarded as part of the culture of etiquette prevalent at the time and not as children's literature in the modern sense. They were part of the old apprenticeship educational system, and the purpose of their production was to teach children (of certain social rank) the behavior appropriate to their status in society. They left no room for further reading, nor did they encourage further education by means of books; moreover, these books lacked the recognition that became part of the conceptual cultural framework of the eighteenth century—the recognition that children needed books of their own that should be different from adult literature and that would suit their needs, at least as understood at the time. Only toward the end of the seventeenth century, with the Puritan writings for children, did children's literature become a culturally recognized field; at that time, special books were issued in order to fulfill the educational needs of children. This development did not signal the demise of courtesy books altogether. They slowly declined or were integrated into the new books for children, serving different functions, as is often the case when new models enter the system.

Thus, children's literature did develop as a new cultural phenomenon. However, this should in no way be regarded as an overnight phenomenon; during this development, elements that already existed in the literary system acquired new functions, in addition to elements that were altogether new. For this reason, the emergence of children's literature should be described as a long process that began more than half a century before children's literature became a distinct field in the publishing world by the middle of the eighteenth century. Obviously, the drastic changes in publishing and in the reading public contributed their share to the emergence of children's literature, but they were a necessary condition, not a sufficient one. What was peculiar to the development of children's literature, as opposed to adult literature, was its linkage to the educational system. This linkage seems to be the prime reason for the delayed appearance of children's literature. This chapter will therefore deal with the causes for the postponement of the emergence of children's literature (as compared to adult) and the circumstances that enabled its emergence.

The Delayed Appearance of Books for Children

Two mutually dependent questions will be raised regarding the delayed beginning of canonized children's literature: Why was there such a delay in the development of children's literature? What changes made the beginning of canonized children's literature possible?

In the first chapter, my discussion focused on the development of the notion of childhood in Western society and the special attention it paid to children's needs, such as clothes, toys, games, and books. The demand for those items for children, especially the demand that children possess their own toys and books, was primarily the result of the radical change in the educational system, which during the seventeenth century passed from an apprenticeship system to a school-based system. The earlier apprenticeship system did not demand the use of books as learning tools, but the school system regarded them as indispensable means for child education. Thus, this new educational system immensely enlarged the number of readers, as the children of tradesmen, middle, and upper classes, previously put to apprenticeship, were now sent to school where they were taught to read. Still, the children of the lowest classes continued to work long hours and in the best of cases enjoyed education only in the Sunday school (whose part in the development of children's literature will be discussed in the next chapter).

Yet, I do not intend to discuss here the development of the educational system, but rather to determine its impact on the development of children's books. The educational system and various educational ideologies responded to the demands of the new reading public, which, in turn, was a by-product of the revolutionary innovation of the school-based system and determined the framework for the first canonized children's books. Thus it was a cyclical process, fueled by the increasing demand from a new reading public and the legitima-

136

tion from within the educational system that made the development of children's literature possible.

Philosophers of education and their followers, who translated the philosophical views into action and actually produced the children's books, had a far-reaching influence on the development of children's books. In fact, their works lay the foundation for almost all canonized children's literature, whether in England, Germany, France, or the United States. Hence, the following universal can be proposed: unlike adult literature, canonized children's literature began to develop in response to the needs of the educational system, the result of which is the strong grip of the educational system on children's literature and the major part it plays in its formulation.

As new ideas about education began to spread, education in the form of the school-based system became more popular and was accordingly redesigned to serve a much larger section of the population. Yet the educational system was initially monopolized, as well as institutionalized, by the religious establishment, which was in the best position to supply the necessary facilities demanded by the newly recognized need for schools. The religious establishment's motivation in forcefully advancing the idea of general literacy lay in the belief that every person should be able to examine the Scriptures by himself. Hence the first schools at which all children had to be taught to read belonged to the church. Moreover, the first canonized books published by the education establishment for children designed to teach both reading and the principles of religion, laid heavy stress on the learning of morals. The basic idea was that through books (necessarily religious in nature) the child would be disciplined along the paths of learning and godliness.

At first, children were given ABC books that included the alphabet, Lord's Prayer, Creed, and Ten Commandments. The ABC books were intended to teach the child to read, but nevertheless were used for teaching morals as well. They commonly opened with the maxim: "In Adam's fall, we sinned all." These books developed into primers, which were particularly widespread in the United States but were also common in Europe. Primers served as the first official reading material for children as evidenced by Adam Martin (born in 1623): "When I was near six years old, one Anne Simpkin . . . bestowed an ABC upon me; a gift in itself exceeding small but . . .

worth more than its weight in gold. For till that time I was all for childish play and never thought of learning . . . and by the help of my brothers and sisters that could read . . . had quickly learned it and the primer also after it. Then of my own accord I fell to reading the bible" (Sloane 1955, 7). In this way, the primers expressed the values that religious education wished to implant. Thus the Puritan-influenced New England primer always stressed the idea of "original sin" and early death because the fundamental Puritan view was that a child is a sinner by nature and his education should guide him along the path of salvation.

As can be seen by the following introductory lines to *The Fathers' Blessing* by William Jole (1674), the main aim of children's books was to arouse in the child the desire for spiritual salvation:

> If you delight to read what I have writ,
> God grant you Grace, that you may practise it.
> Those little children that are wise
> Do fear the Lord and tell no lyes;
> And if their Minds to good they bend
> A Blessing will on them attend.
> The Lord will keep them in his Ways,
> and make them happy all their Days.
>
> (Thwaite 1972, 26)

The books most approved by the Puritans, such as John Bunyan's *Pilgrim's Progress* (1678), which was not written especially for children, and James Janeway's *A Token for Children* (1671), reinforced these major virtues of salvation and early death. Janeway's subtitle explains that his book describes *An Exact Account of the Conversion, Holy and Exemplary Lives, and Joyful Deaths of Several Young Children.* More than anything, this book reveals the nature of the literature considered acceptable for children. However, the Puritan establishment was eventually forced to accept "amusement" as one of the book's components at the beginning of the eighteenth century in order to increase the book's appeal. The scope of children's reading interests developed beyond the Puritan literature, particularly as new models of writing for children based on different educational views entered the scene of canonized literature. These new models emerged from two primary sources: the commercial (see my discussion later in this chapter and in the next one) and the moralist school of education. The moralist school of education developed during the Age of Reason and was soundly based on the writings of Locke and Rousseau. It gradually acquired a status equal to the Puritan approach as an educational philosophy and, in fact, later overtook its place at the center of the canonized literature for children. Unlike the Puritans, who believed children were sinful by nature, the moralists thought that the child was born "tabula rasa" and thus began his life in a state of innocence. The task of education was to shape the child and hence to determine his future as a man. Accordingly, education was allotted a major place in man's life as never before; moreover, since books were considered the main tools in the process of education, a large demand for them arose, resulting in newfound encouragement for children's writers. In this way, the moralist view promulgated by Locke and Rousseau reached many writers for children (mostly women) and opened the way for a change in existing models and the insertion of new ones.

The most significant change initiated by the moralist school lay in the new "raison d'être" of children's books. Unlike the Puritans who taught children to read as a means to better comprehension of the Scriptures, the new school of education considered books as the most appropriate vehicle to integrate Locke's call for "amusement and instruction." Here, reading was regarded as the best means not for mastering the Scriptures, but rather for achieving other educational goals. As one of Locke's disciples, James Burgh, wrote in *The Dignity of Human Nature* (1754): "Nothing will be of more consequence towards the success of a young gentleman's endeavours than his getting early into a right track of reading and study" (Pickering 1981, 20). Ironically enough, the new status allotted to books was in no way apparent from the philosophy of Rousseau, who dismissed the idea of reading except for *Robinson Crusoe;* neither was it apparent from the philosophy of Locke, who pleaded for a more humane approach to the child's education. He was not satisfied with existing children's literature and approved only of *Aesop's Fables, Reynard the Fox,* and the Scriptures: "To this purpose I think *Aesop's Fables* the best, which being stories apt to delight and entertain a child, may yet afford useful reflections to a grown man. And if his memory retain them all his life after, he will not repent to find them there, amongst his manly thoughts and serious business. . . . *Reynard the Fox* is another book, I think, may be made use of to the same purpose" (Darton, 1958, 18).

Locke legitimated the introduction of the model of the fable into children's writing, and numerous editions of *Aesop* were issued, as well as other texts inspired by his "moralist" demand for adequate children's texts. Likewise, the philosophical ideas of Rousseau prompted the insertion of new literary models—and the revision of older ones—into the existing children's literature. Much in the same way that the Puritans integrated religious teachings into their manner books, so the moralists integrated Rousseau and Locke into books and primers of the ABC's. Thus the famous opening of the Puritan primers, reflecting clearly their authors' educational views, "In Adam's fall, we sinned all," was altered in the moralist scheme to something amusing, like "A was an Apple Pie" or "A was an Archer" as in seventeenth-century ABC's, or like the formula that suited both moralists and Newbery's more bourgeois' views:

> A   As you Value your Pence
>   At the *Hole* take your Aim;
>   Chuck all safely in,
>   And you'll win the Game.
>   (*A Little Pretty Pocket-Book*, [21] 71)

Yet the prominent change in the children's literature system and its transformation from a homogeneous to a heterogeneous system was not the result of the revision of existing models, but rather of the creation of new ones. One of these models, the moralist, was deeply rooted in the Rousseauian tradition; a second model, the "informative," was based on both Rousseau's and Locke's views; while the third and most prominent model, the animal story, was supported primarily by Lockean views.

It is not my intention to analyze the differences between Locke's and Rousseau's philosophical views, nor even to discuss their respective views on education. Rather, I point out the way in which the basic conceptions of human nature and the nature of the world, formulated by Locke and Rousseau, were translated into the themes and structure of a new body of literature.

In the case of the first model, the moral story, Rousseau's model of education was translated from an educational model into a literary one. In fact, such a translation was imperative before Rousseau's disciples could begin to write children's books (given Rousseau's rejection of books as a means of education). Thus, in order to produce the desired literature, "Rousseauians" adapted his educational praxis into a literary one. For example, Rousseau suggested the dialogue as an important educational tool; writers inspired by Rousseau thus used dialogue as a basic tool in their work. It is particularly interesting to note that Rousseau's views were integrated into a religious framework, as religious writers believed that knowing nature is a step along the child's way to knowing God. Watts, the most prominent figure in this group of writers, thus wrote in his *Treatise on Education* that if children know that God made "the Heavens and the Earth, and the Birds and the Beasts, and the Trees and Men and Women," they could "be instructed in a Way of easy reasoning in some of the most evident and most necessary Duties which they owe to the Great God whom they see not" (Pickering 1981, 18–19).

The structure of the moral story included a fixed stock of characters and of actions in which they were involved. As suggested by Rousseau's educational model, a commonly found figure was the all-knowing parent, relative, friend, or teacher who could answer all questions and was always at hand to make a profitable lesson out of everything and anything, rendering every experience educational. As Ellenor Fenn stated in her introduction to *The Rational Dame; or, Hints Towards Supplying Prattle for Children* (1790): "Under the inspection of a judicious mother, much knowledge may be acquired whilst little people are enjoying the recreation of a walk; queries arise spontaneously from the scene" (Pickering 1981, 19).

One of the best examples of a translation of Rousseau's views into a literary work was Thomas Day's *Sandford and Merton* (1783–89). This collection of short stories contains two protagonists, Harvey and Tommy—each from a different social class—who are taught by the local clergyman, Mr. Barlow. Their education is mainly carried out through edifying stories of what is good (the simple and the natural) and what is vain (wealth and status). The figure of the teacher, Mr. Barlow, who teaches the inevitable moral through a form of Socratic dialogue, "was a stock figure then or soon afterwards" (Darton 1958, 146) and was the most prominent figure in the "moral stories." For instance, this stock figure appears earlier in Sara Trimmer's *An Easy Introduction to the Knowledge of Nature and Reading the Holy Scriptures, Adapted to the Capacities of Children* (1780), in which two young children are taken for a long walk through the sense-awakening natural world, and later in Mary Wollstonecraft's *Original Stories from Real Life with Conversations Calculated to Regulate the Affections and Form the Mind to Truth and Goodness* (1788).

The other prominent literary models were the "instructive" story and the animal story. The instructive story was a sort of textbook of nature studies, geography, or history, disguised into fiction, and thus combining instruction with amusement. It was not especially intended for instilling morality, but rather for replacing boring textbooks and utilizing the child's leisure time "constructively." Samuel Goodrich used the typical instructive story as a model when writing his Peter Parley series (beginning in 1827), which tells about travel, history, nature, and art (*Tales of Peter Parley About America, Tales of Peter Parley About Europe*); similarly, Jacob Abbott's Rollo series describes a young boy's attempts to cope with the tasks and duties of daily life (*Rollo Learning to Talk, Rollo Learning to Read*). All of these books were extremely popular and sold millions of copies. They established a new model in the children's system that has been popular ever since and even dominates children's literature today (Dick Bruna picture books, Selma Lagerlöf's *The Wonderful Adventures of Nils*, and educational television programs such as *Sesame Street*).

The third model, the animal story, is quite different. What distinguishes this model, and particularly its earlier versions in the eighteenth and nineteenth centuries, is its consistent use of the imaginary. First hinted at by Locke's attitude toward *Aesop's Fables* and *Reynard the Fox*, the idea of imaginary animals as main figures of children's books presented the moralists with a dilemma; their prohibition on imaginary characterization initially precluded the integration of animal talk, animal families, and so forth in children's books.

The solution to this prohibition was again to be found in Locke's ideas, thus dissolving the moralists' difficulty in rationalizing it. Locke contended that the fable constituted the best reading material for children. As a result, a new distinction between the fable, in which the eighteenth-century animal story was contained, and the fairy tale was formulated; the former was within the legitimate bounds of children's literature, while the latter represented the worst possible use of imaginary characterization (see Pickering 1981, 40–104).

In Sara Trimmer's famous *Fabulous Histories* (1786), she argued that children should not believe those stories "containing the real conversation of Birds" but rather should regard them as *"Fables, intended to convey moral instruction applicable to themselves at the same time that they excite compassion and tenderness for those interesting and delightful creatures, on which such wanton cruelties are frequently inflicted, and recommend universal Benevolence"* (Pickering 1981, 20). In fact, the legitimation of the animal story as a fable was enhanced by the implicit subject of the text: its main concentration was not a specific animal itself, but on the relation between that animal and the children. It was believed that a child's attitude toward an animal revealed his real personality—what he was like and what would become of him. In order to construct this relationship, the animal story was built upon a series of events describing children's behavior toward animals or toward their pets; good behavior invariably led to better behavior and culminated in a decent and moral life, while bad behavior led to worse behavior resulting in the eventual death of the child, who grew into a mean and evil adult. This belief was the leading theme in all children's animal stories of the time and appears repeatedly in several texts.

In the story of *The Life and Perambulation of a Mouse* (Kilner 1783), Charles's father claims: "Every action that is cruel and gives pain to *any* living creature, is wicked, and is a sure sign of a *bad* heart. I never knew a man, who was cruel to animals, kind and compassionate towards his fellow-creatures" (Pickering 1981, 22–23). This theme appears again in *Mademoiselle Panache* (Edgeworth 1801), in which unkindness to animals indicates that the girl would not make a good wife. In *The Two Cousins* (Cheap Repository Tracts, 1797), Dick, who is cruel to animals, also mistreats his mother, becomes addicted to gambling, and eventually loses all his mother's money. In *The Adventures of a Silver Penny* (1787), George's torturing of birds precedes his habitual lying and stealing; his bad behavior leaves his father with no choice but to send him to the army, where he gets shot in the head. The pattern surfaces again in *Fabulous Histories* (Trimmer 1786), in which Edward, who tortures animals, continues to do the same to his schoolmates. When he grows up, he "had so hardened his heart, that no kind of distress affected him." Eventually he is killed when a horse that he has beaten throws him. Conversely, his sister Lucy, who unlike Edward has mended her ways, manages to live a long and decent life.

This type of didactic animal story, combining religious views with new educational views, was very popular at the end of the eighteenth century and the beginning of the nineteenth. Some of its most prominent titles were Dorothy Kilner's *The Life and Perambulation of a Mouse* (1783) and Sara Trimmer's *Fabulous Histories; Designed for the Instruction of Children, Respecting Their Treatment of Animals* (1786), later called *The Robins*. The popularity of these stories began to decline only toward the middle of the nineteenth century when the ad-hoc opposition between fables and fairies gave way to the insertion of the imaginative model into the children's system (see chapters 3 and 6). Interestingly enough, it should be noted that animals did not disappear altogether from children's books. In fact, quite the contrary is true—the eighteenth-century model was replaced by a new one in which animals were not meant to serve the same purposes required of them in the eighteenth century. Consequently, animals in the new model constituted the main or exclusive figures of nineteenth- and twentieth-century children's books (the following titles, picked randomly, illustrate this point: North Sterling's *Rascal*, Mary O'Hara's *My Friend Flicka*, Roger Caras's *The Custer Wolf*, Joyce Stranger's *Chia, the Wildcat*, and Robert Lawson's *Rabbit Hill*).

So far, I have discussed the influence of the new educational ideas—and the educational system into which they were integrated—on the development of children's literature, created primarily due to the ideological motivation of its writers. However, the impact of the educational system was quite strong in the case of canonized commercial publishers as well. Although they were not motivated like the moralist writers by ideological considerations, canonized commercial publishers could ill afford to ignore current educational views; children's literature was too strongly linked within culture to the educational system as a whole to allow such. Thus commercial publishers had to take into account prevailing educational views, even at the risk of losing potential commercial success.

They were consequently forced to consider imagination on the whole and fairy tales in particular as unsuitable matter for publication, despite the latter's high commercial value. Ironically, publishers did not hesitate to use characteristic elements of fairy tales in order to enhance the appeal of their books (see next chapter on Newbery's use of these elements). However, they did make it clear to parents and teachers that their books served educational purposes and did not violate the taboo on fairy tales. For instance, when publisher John Marshall advertised *The Histories of More Children Than One; or, Goodness Better Than Beauty,* he assured the public that the book "was totally free from the prejudicial nonsense of *Witches, Fairies, Fortune Tellers, Love and Marriage*" (Pickering 1981, 41). Hence the main condition for a book to be accepted by the canonized children's literature establishment was that it agreed with, or at least did not violate, the basic educational principles. The ideal publication, of course, combined commercial interests with educational interests, as Newbery's books did. In fact, this skilled combination undoubtedly contributed to Newbery's emergence as the first successful commercial publisher.

The pattern of development in children's literature indicates that the educational system not only served as the framework for the creation and legitimation of children's literature, but also determined the stages of its development. The fact that children's literature required the legitimation of the educational establishment, as well as the fact that the educational system served as its primary framework, can thus account for the recurring pattern typical to all beginnings of canonized children's literature. The first official books for children were ABC books, primers, and horn books whose main goal was to teach the child to read for religious purposes and in accordance with a certain religious-educational doctrine. As new educational doctrines evolved, however, children's books began to change as well, acquiring widespread appeal and catalyzing the new field of commercial publishing for children. As a result, the canonized system lost its homogeneous nature and became heterogeneous (moral stories, animal stories, instructive stories, primers, readers). Eventually, it became stratified and subject to competition and struggle between the various models.

A Test Case: Hebrew Children's Literature

As a test case for analyzing a parallel historical pattern, I will discuss Hebrew children's literature, chosen primarily because it is historically exceptional—Hebrew children's literature was "abnormal" literature as far as its language and territorial existence were concerned since it did not address children in their native language and developed in various territories. All the same, a repetition of the entire process described above may be seen, in spite of its development almost one hundred years after European children's literature had become a recognized and important field in publishing. If the same pattern can be discerned in the development of such a peculiar case, then it may indeed exemplify more than any other case the model for the emergence of children's literature, since its analysis focuses on the cultural circumstances required for the development of a given children's literature at a given point in time.

When the development of Hebrew children's literature is examined, three questions should be raised: Why the delay? Why the strong dependency on German children's literature? Why was the incipient stage of development of the German model imitated? Despite its solid dependency on German literature, Hebrew children's literature did not use the inventory current at the time in the German system as might have been expected, but rather went back almost one hundred years in order to repeat the entire developmental process of German children's literature. This can be explained, in spite of the obviously different conditions of eighteenth- and nineteenth-century Europe, by the cultural situation for Hebrew children's literature and its similarities to eighteenth-century German children's literature, as it also needed, like the German, the framework and legitimation of the educational system. However, unlike German children's literature, Hebrew children's literature only managed to liberate itself from this framework at a very late stage, and only then did it become a "normal" fully stratified system.

THE STATE OF HEBREW CHILDREN'S LITERATURE

By the time Hebrew children's literature had begun to develop, European children's literature had already reached a fairly advanced

stage and was rapidly approaching its so-called "golden age." The
delay in the development of Hebrew children's literature was deeply
rooted in the complicated status of the Hebrew language itself and its
multiterritorial existence. These unique conditions, to a large extent,
determined the character of Hebrew literature as a whole and also
account for the dependent position of Hebrew children's literature
on the German (see Even-Zohar 1974, 1978c, 1978e, 1978f).

Moreover, these particular conditions also acted as an ideological
basis for Hebrew children's literature for over a century and determined its structure and the nature of its inventory. In fact, it was only
in the late 1940s, when the commercial factor began to play a central
role in the publishing of children's books, that Hebrew children's
literature managed to liberate itself from that ideological basis. Before and even during the "Israeli" period, publishing of Hebrew children's books was hardly profitable (except for a short time in Eastern
Europe), but was motivated by the values it represented (as was the
case with most children's book publishing in Europe in the eighteenth century). As a result, the system of Hebrew children's literature was for a long time a defective system lacking some of its member parts (see Even-Zohar 1978e), leading to a semitaboo on non-
canonized texts[1] and creating a demand for other didactic texts.
However, while these ideological considerations did impose various
limitations on the texts, they were also the very factors that actually enabled the creation of Hebrew children's literature within the context
of the Jewish cultural Enlightenment movement in Germany, from
around the end of the eighteenth century until the middle of the nineteenth, when the center of Hebrew culture moved to Eastern Europe.[2]

[1] As Professor Shmeruk claims, children probably read popular Yiddish literature
because Yiddish functioned as the non-canonized system for Hebrew literature. At
least part of the development of Hebrew children's literature can be explained in terms
of its need to compete with Yiddish reading, but unfortunately, very little research has
been done on this issue.

[2] When Hebrew children's literature in Europe is discussed, books published in the
German period are rarely mentioned. This can be justified normatively, as the first
texts for children did not have any later value as "living texts" for the reading public.
From a historical prespective, however, one cannot ignore the German period, not
only because it was a formative period, but also because the historical processes and
procedures of the German period largely determine both the character of the later
periods and their historical options.

Unlike European children's literature, which had to wait only for the emergence and crystallization of the concept of the child before child-oriented books could be written, Hebrew children's literature had to wait for a total reform in the concepts of Jewish society's educational values before Hebrew books for children could be written. Consequently there was a delay of over one hundred years from the time the first European books for children were written.

Hebrew children's literature became possible not because of the emergence of European children's literature, but because of the emergence of a new social and cultural movement—the Jewish Enlightenment movement, whose main goals were cultural, especially in the field of education. This movement created for the first time in Jewish society a demand for special books for children, which, in turn, created both the framework and motivation for Hebrew children's literature. The earliest writers were enlightened Jews who utilized their texts to disseminate their movement's ideology. Most ideas of the Jewish Englishment, especially those concerning education, were rooted in the German Enlightenment.[3] The Jewish movement adopted not only the German views about nature, man, and aesthetics as ultimate views, but also tried to apply the "Philanthropinismus" ideas on education to Jewish schools. In fact the movement's followers built a whole system of new schools based on these views, in Breslau, Dessau, Hamburg, and Frankfurt.[4]

This new education system naturally needed appropriate books for expounding the new ideas; selection of the texts was made accordingly. The first Hebrew books for children were primarily oriented toward those children studying in schools of the Jewish Enlightenment movement or to those children whose parents favored its ideas. The books, most of them readers (like the first European children's books), were aimed at teaching the child the German language, imparting to him knowledge of the world, and socializing him properly.

[3] Mendelssohn and Basedow corresponded and Mendelssohn even recommended that the Jews support Basedow in publishing *Elementarwerk*. He also persuaded the Jews to donate 500 talers for the foundation of Philanthropin in Dessau (Eliav 1960).

[4] Jewish schools were the first to follow strictly Philanthropin views on education. Investigation into those views should be directed primarily to the Jewish schools; not until the middle of the nineteenth century did the Germans build their first modern schools, based on Pestalozzi's ideas (Eliav 1960).

Because of the ideological relations between the Jewish and German enlightenment movements, German children's literature was not only a natural frame of reference, but also an ideal to be imitated, albeit a century later. The German system was imitated in four ways. The historical development of German children's literature served as a model for the development of Hebrew children's literature. Most texts for children were either translations of German texts, or adaptations based on those texts. German children's literature served as a mediating system for the Hebrew system; texts translated from other systems, like French or English, were usually translated via the German. The few original texts (either plays, poems or fables), written at the time, were based so completely on the German model that it is very difficult to distinguish between original and translated texts.

THE MODEL OF DEVELOPMENT

By the middle of the nineteenth century, European children's literature had managed to liberate itself from the sole hegemony of the didactic approach, becoming more stratified and generically more complicated. Hebrew children's literature did not adjust itself to this latter stage of development of European children's literature, but rather to the initial stages; and thus the first Hebrew texts for children were ABC books and readers, followed by moral books, fables, and some plays.

There were two reasons for the repetition of this whole process: the first involved a certain demand, the other a certain legitimation. The reading public of Hebrew children's literature was created by the Enlightenment movement; consequently, the first books had to respond to its demands, which included certain assumptions about the child's education. The Enlightenment movement's ideas served also as the legitimation given to the books produced. This particular legitimation assumed that it was impossible to produce children's books simply for literature's sake. This is why Hebrew children's literature in Germany never went beyond what might be called "the didactic age" of children's literature, not accepting the new models prevalent at the time in the children's system and only taken on those which were rooted in Philanthropinismus views, such as fables and moral texts.

The German case served as a model both for stages of development and for textual models. The first Hebrew ABC and readers were based on German readers as far as pedagogic ideas and textual content were concerned. For instance, they adopted the German method of teaching the alphabet (despite the obvious differences between the two languages), by starting with texts comprising basic vowels and consonants and gradually moving to more and more difficult texts, as in the Ben-Zeev reader (1820):

> To-ra Zi-va La-nu Mo-she Mo-ra-sha Khi-lat Ya-acov: Shma Bni Mu-sar A-vi-cha veal Ti-tosh To-rat I-me-cha. (Ben-Zeev 1820, 24)[5]
>
> [Moshe bequeathed the torah to us, the tradition to the people of Jacob. My son, hear the instruction of thy father, and foresake not the law of thy mother.]

Like German readers, Hebrew readers contained poems, morals, and fables, as well as various texts about nature, geography, man, and society, such as the following about the structure of society:

> And the other people in the state of the Kingdom: officers, noblemen, aristocrats, wisemen, writers, teachers, and priests. Sages write books of science and knowledge. Teachers teach the sciences to their students in academies. Priests preach the Torah and morality, and guide the people in religion and divine service in the House of Prayer. . . . Happy is the boy who, in his youth, industriously studies a science or craft and when he grows up this ensures that he will not be hungry nor suffer a lack. But the lazy boy who, in his youth, does not study anything will grow up with nothing in his hands to earn a living and will remain poor and wretched for the rest of his life. (Ben-Zeev 1820, 57)

All texts were either explicitly committed to Enlightenment ideas, or were chosen because they could be accommodated to them. Writers were even willing to change traditional aphorisms in order to adjust them to these new views, as illustrated by one of the most popular readers of the time, *Mesilat ha-Limud* (written by Ben-Zeev). In one chapter, Ben-Zeev introduces sayings from the Talmud, in spite of

---

5 Translations of Hebrew examples are literal.

the fact that the Enlightenment movement, generally speaking, was hostile to the Talmud; for followers of the Enlightenment, the Talmud and the Mishna reflected everything they rejected in Judaism. Nevertheless, Ben-Zeev did include some Talmudic sayings (perhaps in order to attract Orthodox Jews). However, by placing them with Greek proverbs under the category of "Wise Men," he presented them as a part of the general humanistic heritage. Thus, the Greek sayings were granted thirty pages, whereas only a page and a half were devoted to the Talmudic and included only those sayings that suited the ideas of the Enlightenment movement, such as: "So said the sages: A man should always be involved with his friends, should not laugh among the weeping, nor weep among the merry, nor be awake among the sleeping nor sleep among the wakers, nor stand among the seated nor sit among the standing, nor change his friends' manners" (Ben-Zeev 1820, 219). In at least one case, the saying was even altered. The famous saying, "In three ways a man is distinguished: his pocket, his glass and his anger," was altered to "In four ways the sages are distinguished: their pocket, their glass, their anger and their dress" (Ben-Zeev 1820, 219).

The Hebrew system's tendency to rely heavily on the German is perhaps best manifested in Bible teaching. The Jewish Enlightenment movement's positive attitude toward the Bible can be traced to the great deference and respect displayed toward the Bible by the Germans and later consolidated by Mendelssohn's translation. However, Bible teaching was strongly oriented toward fulfilling the aims of the Enlightenment movement. The translation was initially used as a means of studying both German and Hebrew. Soon thereafter the idea of teaching the Bible itself was abandoned and replaced with the biblische Geschichte, the teaching of the history of the Bible, as can be seen from the following example:

At the end of seventy years of the Babylonian exile, the Lord remembered his people and brought them back to his land. And they settled again, as they had the first time and built again the House of the Chosen and settled in peace for another four hundred years. However, again this time, they did not keep God's law and refused to walk in his path. Although they had seen and known bad times in Babylon, morality they did not learn. When the Lord saw what evil they made of his law and how they broke their covenant, he sold them to the kings of the surrounding peoples. Then came the Romans, who fought them and took their country and burned the Holy City of Jerusalem and the House of God. They drove away the people from their land and put an end to their kingdom and scattered them among the Gentiles in exile all over the world. Since then and till now, we are scattered among the Gentiles in the four corners of the earth. Strangers everywhere with no estate neither a vineyard nor a field. (Ben-Zeev 1820, 112)

Thus, in spite of the attraction that Bible teaching could have held for orthodox parents, the Jewish Enlightenment movement preferred to follow the German example because of the high status attributed to the German culture.

The prime aim of the Jewish Enlightenment was the desire to merge with German culture; its leaders believed this could be achieved through acquisition of the German language. That this was so can be easily attested to by the graphic format of the texts for children. Most texts were written in both Hebrew and German; the Hebrew was utilized in order to teach German and German to teach Hebrew, though Hebrew was, in essence, a dead language at the time. There were three formats for printing Hebrew and German: Hebrew opposite German in Latin letters, Hebrew opposite German in Hebrew letters, and Hebrew with German in Hebrew letters below.[6]

To sum up, the German model of development was followed by the Hebrew model because of similar legitimations given to both at their respective formative stages. The Hebrew system's use of the German as a frame of reference determined not only its stages of development, but also the nature of its texts—original and translated.

TRANSLATION AND ADAPTATION

Texts, in particular those of poetry and fables, were chosen for adaptation and translation either because they were works of German Enlightenment writers (considered by Jewish writers as the informal representatives of German children's literature) or because of the

[6] The last format might have had a special intention: to mislead Orthodox Jews, who were used to reading texts written in Hebrew and Yiddish in this form (see Shmeruk 1978).

implicit Enlightenment attitudes and values they embodied, as can be seen in the following poem by Schiller, which was undoubtedly chosen for translation because of the importance attached to "wisdom":

Successful man success deserted
Willingly gave her hand to wisdom
To you I'll give all my goodness
From now on, be my love.
The honor of my wealth and treasure I gave to him
None is as big as him in the whole world
But his thirsty lust I have not yet quenched
I was called mean and stingy.
Come my sister we will make an eternal covenant
During the plowing season it will not be tempted to throw fennel.
In your bosom I'll put the glory of my greatness
Both will be satisfied by my fertile property.
Wisdom laughed hearing her words
And wiped the sweat from her face
Your lover has gone to take his life
Forgive his crimes. I can live quietly without you.

(Ben-Zeev 1820, 30)

Even in the case of fables, translations dominated, although original fables did exist in the Hebrew inventory and could easily have been used. In the section dedicated to fables in *Mesilat ha-Limud*, the most popular reader, there were twenty-one translations of German Enlightenment writers, such as Albrecht von Haller (1708–77), Friedrich von Hagedorn (1708–54), and Christian Fürchtegott Gellert (1715–96);[7] only thirteen were original (some had already been published in *Ha-Measef*, the adult periodical of the Jewish Enlightenment).[8]

[7] Only Gellert was known at the time as a writer of fables for children. The other two seem to have been known only as adult writers. They may have been adopted by the Hebrew children's system via the Hebrew adult system.

[8] Although the strong connections between the two children's systems were indispensable for the Hebrew system, the transfer from German children's literature to Hebrew children's literature was not always direct; in certain cases the transfer went via the adult system and vice versa. Hebrew children's literature served in some cases as the connecting system (though peripheral) between the Hebrew and the German

It is the strong orientation of Hebrew children's literature toward the German Enlightenment that explains why Campe, a distinguished Enlightenment writer, was so very popular among Hebrew translators. The entire number of books translated into Hebrew during the German period did not exceed fifty, yet almost all Campe's books were translated into Hebrew, some even more than once—*Robinson der Jüngere* was translated into Hebrew three times, as was *Die Entdeckung von America*. His moral book *Theophron* was translated more than five times. Campe enjoyed such high status in Hebrew children's literature that his books remained popular among Hebrew readers even after the German center had declined and the cultural center had moved to Eastern Europe. Hence, the German system for children continued to serve as a mediating system, even in Eastern Europe.

THE GERMAN SYSTEM AS A MEDIATING SYSTEM

The German system served as a mediating system for the general Hebrew literary polysystem, continuing to do so for children's books even after the Russian system had taken over as the mediating system for adult literature (see Even-Zohar 1978c). Authors of other national systems, like Stephanie Genlis and Daniel Defoe, were translated through the German. Genlis was translated into German mainly because of the Rousseauian views expressed in her books, which probably accounts for the fact that her work was translated as well into Hebrew. Defoe's *Robinson Crusoe*, however, is more complicated and probably became as popular a children's book as it did (and the model for a whole genre, the *Robinsonnade*) thanks to Campe's adaptation. Campe decided upon adapting the original Robinson into *Robinson der Jüngere* on the strength of Rousseau's remark in *Émile* that it was the only book he would give to his son. However, in order to conform to Rousseau's views, Campe needed to greatly revise the

---

adult systems. The dual functioning of the Hebrew adult and children's systems in the interference relations is connected with the blurred borders of each system. Most of the writers for children wrote for adults as well and often published the same text in periodicals for adults and in books for children. This fact is bound up both with the low status of the writer for children and with the still-blurred status of children's literature that is typical of the beginning of children's literature everywhere in Europe.

text. Moreover, the revised text had to be further adapted in order to suit the ideas of the Jewish Enlightenment. The Hebrew translation of *Robinson der Jüngere* was used in one version (David Zamoshch's) to convey the Jewish Enlightenment ideas on productivization, the importance of studying and understanding the world, and love of mankind. Thus, the following conversation between father (narrator) and son is used to teach both geography and good manners:

> *Issachar:* What are the travellers of Genoa?
> *The father:* Ask Gad and he'll tell you.
> *Gad:* Do you know there is a state called the Land of the South, and it has a shore.
> *Issachar:* A shore?
> *Gad:* The Land close to the sea. Look at my globe. This strip of land is called the Genoa shore.
> *The father:* The people who go there for their business are called the travellers of Genoa. (Zamoshch 1824, 12)

Meanwhile the following passage is meant to teach love for all mankind:

> *Shimon:* Were they the people of Hamburg?
> *The father:* Should we help only the people of our own country? Is that what you mean, my son? If someone from America should fall into the river in front of our eyes, would we ask where he comes from? Would not we save him from death? These people do have hearts, just as we do, although they are neither from Hamburg, nor are they Europeans. They were not Christians, but Muslems of Izmir in Asia.
> *Shimon:* That I did not know, that Muslems are of kind heart.
> *The father:* You should know that among every people and in every state there are good people, just as there are in every people and every generation the bad and the reckless. (Zamoshch 1824, 10)

By translating from the German, Hebrew writers accomplished at least two objects: they were able to use texts that had already acquired legitimation and could therefore be easily legitimized by the Hebrew system and they managed to adopt the main components of a system considered as ideal for imitation and thus laid the groundwork for acceptance of the new system. Just how strong this need to

155

follow the German model was can be discerned in the case of original Hebrew texts.

ORIGINAL TEXTS BASED ON GERMAN MODELS

At the outset, original Hebrew texts for children were few, and the distinction between the original texts and translations blurred. As translated texts were so common, translators did not even bother citing the name of the original author; at times, it is almost impossible to determine whether a text is original or translated (a good example is *Mishle Agur* by Shalom Hacohen).

Most original texts were based on and constructed in the same way as German texts (readers and Bible stories). In fact, the dominance of the German model is evident even in original fiction. But since original writing was rare, and translations were more easily accepted, writers sometimes felt reluctant to acknowledge themselves as the authors, preferring instead to present the text either as a contemporary translation or as an adaptation of an ancient text (ancient Greek and Hebrew texts were popular at the time). This was the case with the fables of a certain Satenof, who preferred to attribute his fables to Asaf Ben Brachia (a psalmist mentioned in the *Chronicles*). When accused of plagiarism, he defended himself by saying that writers commonly stole and never bothered to accredit true authorship,[9] while he (poor chap!) was being accused of stealing from himself and attributing it to someone else (see Ofek 1979). In any case, Satenof's fables are still quite close to the model of Enlightenment fables and are very similar to those that were translated. The explanation for this similarity lies in one of two possibilities: either the Germans themselves, like Satenof, tried to imitate ancient formulas or Satenof deliberately tried to imitate the German model in order to make his original acceptable.

Thus, because German children's literature functioned as a frame of legitimation for Hebrew children's literature, the Hebrew system fol-

---

[9] Although the habit of not citing the source text was very common, writers were often accused of "stealing" texts. Ben-Zeev, for instance, who wanted to defend himself in advance, declared that he attached the names of the original writers in order to avoid any attack on himself.

lowed its model of development (and used its inventory) to such an extent that it was almost entirely composed of translated or pseudo-translated texts. Moreover, the peripheral literary system preserved its contact with the German long after the adult system had disconnected itself.

The short examination of the model of development of Hebrew children's literature manifests the strong linkage between children's literature and ideology and the extent of its dependence on the educational system. Yet in order to focus on the relations between educational doctrines and historical processes in the children's system, this scheme deliberately ignores, for methodological reasons, the function of popular literature in the development of children's literature. It should be clear, however, that although this separation is methodologically valuable, a full analysis of the development of children's literature cannot be undertaken without considering the function of popular literature. The next chapter is devoted to this issue.

Texts

Ben-Zeev, Yehuda Leyb. 1820. *Bet Ha-Sefer.* Part 1, *Mesilat ha-Limud.* Part 2, *Limude ha-mešarim.* Vienna: Anton Schmidt.

[Campe, J. H.]. 1824. *Robinson der Yingere,* Eyn lezebukh fir kinder. Ins Hebräishe ibertragen von David Zamoshch. Breslau: Sulzbach.

[Campe, J. H.]. 1819. *Tokehot Musar.* German front page: *Sittenbüchlein für Kinder,* Zur allgemeinen Schul-encyklopädie gehörig. Von J. H. Campe. Ins Hebräische ubersezt von David Zamoshch. Breslau: Sulzbach.

[Cohen], Šalom b.r.y.k. from Mezrich. 1799. *Sefer Misle Agur.* Part 1, *Oder moralisches fabel-buch.* Berlin: in der Orientalischen Buchdruckerei.

Rothstein, Fayvil ha-Levi. 1844. *Moda Li-bne-ha-neurim.* German front page: *Der Jugendfreund, Oder Der dreifache Faden.* Hebräisch und Deutsch von Ph. Rothstein. Königsberg.

[Satenof, Isaak]. 1788. *Misle Asaf.* Berlin. German colophon: Die Weisheits Sprüche Asaphs herausgegeben von R. Isaak Satenof.

Zamoshch, David. 1834. *Eš Dat: tsum unterrikht im lezen und anfangsgrinde der religion.* Tsum iberzetsen oys dem hebräishen ins daytše firdi izraelitische Jugend. Breslau: Sulzbach.

Chapter Seven

Stratification of a System

 It is almost impossible to discuss the development of children's literature without accounting for the function of chapbooks. Despite the fact that histories of children's literature almost completely ignore them (see Townsend 1977, Darton 1958, Thwaite 1972), chapbooks were the core of seventeenth-century popular literature and served not only as reading material for children but also as an important catalyst in the development of children's books. Indeed, every stage in the development of children's literature can be explained in terms of the competition between the canonized children's system and chapbooks.

As determined in previous chapters, one of the results of the new notion of childhood was the emergence of a new education system and an enormous expansion in size and character of literate circles. A new, previously unknown reading public—children (and classes other than the highbrow)—came into being, gradually creating a demand for children's books, which could not yet be supplied. The lack of almost any official books for children meant that children adapted for their own use what already existed: chapbooks. These books, until then read mainly by the poor, were now read by both the poor and children. At the same time, the literary, as well as the religious and educational establishments, gradually became aware not only of the specifically new phenomenon of children reading, but also of the nature of their reading material. Not surprisingly, the reactions of the various establishments were identical: each felt an urgent need to compete with and supersede chapbooks. This competition was a strong motivating force for all establishments that, from the eighteenth century, became involved in the production of books for children, albeit each from a different point of departure. The first to react to chapbooks were commercial publishers, who recognized the high commercial poten-

158

tial of a market which hitherto had not been explored. They realized that as long as the education system's tenets were not violated, production of children's books could become quite profitable; children and their parents were clearly willing to pay the price of books. Hence, commercial publishers tried to produce children's books that would be as attractive as chapbooks, but that would still be acceptable to parents and teachers.

Concomitantly, the other forces involved with publishing for children could not lag behind if they were to survive. Both the religious and moralist schools considered chapbooks corrupting and unsuitable for children; yet they realized that they could not prevent children either from reading, now a widespread phenomenon, or from acquiring inappropriate material. Thus, the only way left for them to fight chapbooks was to replace them, which could be achieved only by offering children alternative reading material.

Although the various establishments involved in the production of books for children had different motivations and produced children's books in order to achieve different goals, they did share one common denominator: all tried to compete with chapbooks. By offering better prices or by borrowing literary elements commonly found in chapbooks themselves (similar plots, stock characters), they increased the appeal of their books. As a result of this effort and the newly stimulated competition that stemmed from it, publishers of chapbooks were forced to improve their products as well. Accordingly, they began to publish chapbooks especially designed for children that were better illustrated and produced.

This then is the scheme of the historical process by which the literary polysystem became more stratified. In addition to the forces of the education system that made the creation of canonized children's literature possible and were responsible for the increase in the number of readers, new opposing forces emerged in the literary polysystem. That is, in addition to the already existing opposition between canonized and non-canonized literature, a new opposition between adult and children's readership developed out of the popular system. The new system resulting from this opposition, the autonomous children's literary system, soon became stratified itself; already by the middle of the eighteenth century it had developed canonized and non-canonized subsystems.

The State of the System

Prior to the seventeenth century there were few books specifically produced for children; moreover, the few children who knew how to read, read adult literature. Most children's exposure to reading was provided in shared reading sessions with adults. For example, in one of the early editions of *Gesta Romanorum,* a woodcut shows a whole family gathered around the fire on a winter night reading stories to pass the time. There is evidence of other shared stories, such as traveler's tales, Caxton's books, and Ovid's *Metamorphosis,* which were not intended for children at all. In fact, as Brockman observes, the secondary importance of children is revealed by "a manuscript illumination of Ovid reading the *Metamorphosis* which includes in the outdoor audience, discreetly to one side, a pair of children" (Brockman 1982, 3). Some stories, like *Aesop's Fables* and *The History of Reynard the Fox,* later became tales exclusively for children, as the children's canonized system seized and monopolized them. Undoubtedly, this process could have occurred only after the stories had gained the acceptance of the educational establishment.

Thus, almost three hundred years after the invention of the printing press, children's books—mainly ABC's and "courtesy" books—were few in number and were produced neither systematically nor steadily. The few children's books published prior to the seventeenth century (and written in the vernacular)[1] therefore acquired only a limited audience, comprising two types of children readers: those who would hold a suitable place in "good" society or those who, in one way or another, would serve the church. At the beginning of the seventeenth century, however, as education spread and literate circles expanded, a new reading public emerged, creating a large demand for children's books. This demand could not, as yet, be supplied by the educational establishment involved in publishing for children, in spite of the legitimation that reading had recently gained; as noted in the previous chapter, education was tightly controlled by the church and was intended for "serious" educational purposes only. Thus,

---

[1] They introduced the vernacular, which then became the language and distinguishing feature of children's literature. Whereas a portion of canonized literature for adults was still written in Latin, books for children were written or translated into the vernacular from the very beginning.

reading was viewed as acceptable as the gateway to higher religious enlightenment, but absolutely not for entertainment or pleasure.

A new function was therefore created in the literary system—the function of supplying reading material to a new reading public—which existing elements of the official system could not fulfill. Officially, the first to fill this vacuum were primers and some religious treatises; unofficially, however, the task was taken over by chapbooks. During the seventeenth and even at the beginning of the eighteenth century, the absence of books specially produced for children meant that they still had to borrow reading material from the adult library in order to satisfy their reading needs. This material consisted mainly of chapbooks, which had reached a sizable output by the eighteenth century.

SOURCES FOR CHAPBOOKS

Chapbooks, paper-covered books sold by peddlers and hawkers, became the most popular reading material of the seventeenth and eighteenth centuries. These commercially successful books were heavily influenced by the following sources: ballad sheets (*Children in the Wood, The Death and Burial of Cock Robin*), sometimes rewritten in prose; Elizabethan jestbooks (*Cambridge Jests, or Wit's Recreation; Poets Jest, or Mirth in Abundance*); romance and chivalry stories (*Guy, Earl of Warwick; Bevis of Southampton; Hector, Prince of Troy; Valentine and Orson; Robin Hood*); adventure stories (*Johnny Armstrong of Westmoreland, Captain James Hind*); sensational and supernatural stories (*The History of Dr. John Faustus, The History of Learned Fryar Bacon, The Witch of the Woodlands, The Foreign Travels of Sir John Mandeville, Containing an Account of Remote Kingdoms, Countries, Rivers, Castles, etc. Together with a Description of Giants, Pigmies and Various Other People and Odd Deformities*). A smaller number of chapbooks were adaptations and abridgments of books that enjoyed current popularity, such as Defoe's *Robinson Crusoe* and *Moll Flanders* and Swift's *Gulliver's Travels*. Chapbooks also included fairy tales (*Blue Beard, Jack the Giant Killer, Little Red Riding Hood, Puss in Boots*) that were later deemed unsuitable for children, as it was thought that they would hinder the healthy development of sensitive young children.

161

PRODUCTION OF CHAPBOOKS

Writers of chapbooks had to fit texts into a certain format, usually between sixteen and twenty-four pages. This was done either by shortening or lengthening a given text, or by adding woodcut illustrations, which until that time had not been used in texts produced for children. These particular specifications of the chapbook proved to be most agreeable to the chapbooks' intended audience, poor adults, who also were attracted to the chapbook's low price. In fact, the layout design and price of the chapbooks allowed them to become the most popular source of reading material during the seventeenth century.

A. E. Dobbs describes the widespread appearance of chapbooks as reading matter: "In the provinces—even in the larger towns—there was a great scarcity of first-rate literature, a disproportionate amount of space being occupied by tales of magic and adventure, lives of highway men, ephemeral histories, love stories, valentines, prophetic almanacs, 'godly and other patters,' slip-songs, children's books and antiquated treatises on various subjects sold in numbers four sheets for a penny" (Neuburg 1972, 2). And Cotton Mather wrote in his diary of 27 September 1713: "I am informed that the Minds and Manners of many People about the Countrey are much corrupted by foolish Songs and Ballads, which the Hawkers and Peddlars carry into all parts of the Countrey" (Townsend 1977, 24). James Lackington, the bookseller, details in his memoirs published in 1803 the extent of chapbook dissemination, particularly among the poor, in the eighteenth century:

> I cannot help observing, that the sale of books in general has increased prodigiously within the last twenty years. According to the best estimate I have been able to make, I suppose that more than four times the number of books are sold now than were sold twenty years since. The poorer sort of farmers and even the poor country people in general, who before that period spent their winter evenings in relating stories of witches, ghosts, hobgoblings &c. now shorten the winter nights by hearing their sons and daughters read tales, romances &c, and on entering their houses you may see Tom Jones, Roderic Random and other entertaining books stuck up in their bacon-racks &c. (Neuburg 1972, 14).

During the seventeenth and eighteenth centuries, however, the mass-produced chapbooks moved out of the somewhat exclusive domain of adult literature and became a major source of reading material for children. This occurred not only as a result of their low price, but also (and perhaps more importantly) due to the absence of other sources of reading material for children. Thus from the seventeenth century until the middle of the eighteenth, people of lower classes and children shared books—just as they shared other cultural items such as clothes, costumes, games, and education (see Ariès 1962). But the class differentiation between rich and poor, so markedly characteristic of adult culture, did not carry over to children's culture—at least not until the middle of the eighteenth century. As Neuburg claims, noting the chapbooks' transcendent appeal: "In the eighteenth century, in the absence of juvenile books, chapbooks were widely read by the children of well-to-do families" (1972, 5). One of the children of those well-to-do families was Sir Richard Steele's godson, whose reading material was described by Steele on the pages of *Tatler* (1709, no. 5) in the following way:

> I perceived him a very great historian in Aesop's Fables; but he frankly declared to me his mind "that he did not delight in that learning, because he did not believe that they were true," for which reason I found that he had very much turned his studies for about a twelve-months past, into the lives and adventures of Don Bellianis of Greece, Guy of Warwick, The Seven Champions and other historians of that age. . . . He would tell you the mismanagements of John Hickathrift, find fault with the passionate temper in Bevis of Southampton, and loved Saint George for being the champion of England; and by this means had his thoughts insensibly moulded into the notion of discretion, virtue and honour." (Muir 1969, 23; Darton 1958, 33)

Other adults also referred to reading chapbooks in their childhood—and in quite a fashionable manner, as did Boswell or Goethe. In Boswell's *Journal* of 10 July 1763, he described his visit to the "old printer-office in Bow Churchyard kept by Dicey": "There are ushered into the world the literature *Jack and the Giants, The Seven Wise Men of Gotham* and other story-books which in my dawning years amused me as much as *Rasselas* does now" (Thwaite 1972, 41). In *Dichtung und Wahrheit*, Goethe wrote: "We children therefore had the good fortune to find daily on the little table in front of the second-hand bookseller's doorway these precious remnants of the Middle Ages: *Eulenspiegel, The Four Sons of Aymon, Fair Melusine, Kaiser Octavian, Fortunatus*—the whole bunch, right down to *The Wandering Jew;* everything was there for us" (Hürlimann 1967, xiii–xv).

Once the book trade came to realize the commercial potential of the children's market, as indicated by the expanding popularity of chapbooks, it tried to appeal specifically to those who could afford to buy other books—the bourgeois and the upper classes. As a result, a new gap was created in the reading material of upper and lower class children, a gap that was widened by the educational establishment's prohibition of chapbooks. In such a way, chapbooks became the overt reading material solely of the poor, though it is evident that children of higher classes continued to read them secretly. Yet in quite a short time, chapbooks became underground literature for children of all classes, as the religious establishment began to pay attention to the reading material and education of the poor as well.

THE ESTABLISHMENT'S ATTITUDE TOWARD CHAPBOOKS

Neither the religious nor the educational establishments were as delighted by the mass reading of chapbooks by children as Boswell or Goethe were in their nostalgic childhood reminiscences. On the contrary, the more important the child's education (and consequently his reading matter) became, the less the educational establishment approved of chapbook reading. As early as 1708, an anonymous writer of the *History of Genesis* wrote about the dangers in reading chapbooks: "How often do we see Parents prefer 'Tom Thumb,' 'Guy of Warwick,' or some such foolish Book, before the Book of Life! Let not your children read those vain Books, profane Ballads and filthy songs. Throw away all fond and amorous Romances and fabulous Histories of Giants, the bombast Atchievements of Knight Errantry, and the like; for these all fill the Heads of Children with vain, silly and idle imaginations" (Avery 1975, 33; Neuburg 1968, 19–20). A few years earlier, in 1702, Thomas White likewise warned his readers in his school book: "When thou canst read, read no Ballads and foolish Books, but the Bible" (Neuburg 1968, 18–19).

These were just the first people to denounce and fight chapbooks.

From the middle of the eighteenth century, a war on chapbooks was declared mainly by the religious establishment, which regarded them as *the* source of evil. Philip Dormer, the fourth earl of Chesterfield and "patron" of Johnson, wrote to his son in 1740: "The reading of romances is a most frivolous occupation, and time merely thrown away. The old romances, written two or three hundred years ago, such as Amadis of Gaul, Orlando the Furious, and others, were stuffed with enchantments, magicians, giants, and such sort of impossibilities" (Darton 1958, 47). The establishment's fight against chapbooks was not limited to propagandistic articles. At the same time, there was a concerted effort to overcome chapbooks by offering children alternative reading material; ironically, this effort in itself played an important role in the development of the children's system. But even more crucial for the growth of children's literature was the discovery by the commercial publishing world of the hitherto unexplored potential of the children's reading market. Thus the existence of chapbooks and the fact that they were read by children were the the prime motivations for the momentous change in the field of publishing for children. The fight against chapbooks, for whatever reason (and not least important, the commercial), also contributed to the initial stratification of the children's system, as well as to its transformation from a homogeneous to a heterogeneous system.

Commerical Reaction: Manipulation of Chapbook Elements

The fact that children were reading chapbooks proved to eighteenth-century commerical publishers that there was a section of the reading public whose needs were hardly being administered to. Until the eighteenth century, there was not a single publisher catering specifically to the children's market. However, in the eighteenth century, publishers realized this potential and tried to compete with chapbooks, mainly by inserting identical elements into their books. For instance, publishers like Thomas Boreman and Mary Cooper, who published books with an educational appeal, nevertheless utilized chapbook elements, especially in their titles. Boreman published books entitled *Gigantick Histories*, while Cooper published books entitled *The Child's New Plaything* and short versions of *Guy of Warwick* and *Reynard the Fox.* Neither had much success (the list of Boreman's subscribers never extended beyond 649 and even decreased to 106), apparently because they never took on steady and regular publishing for children.

The first commercial publisher to be successful in building a solid business of publishing for children was John Newbery. It might be said that Newbery's success reflected what one writer, named Shenstone, wrote to his publisher when his fables project was being considered: "A book of this kind, once established, becomes an absolute estate for many years; and brings in at least as certain and regular returns" (Darton 1958, 23). Unlike other commercial publishers for children at the time, Newbery understood that penetration of the market must be constant and regular. He also understood that, in order to compete with chapbooks, he had to appeal to the child; but, in order to have an advantage over the chapbook, he must not violate the values of the teachers and the parents. Thus he was not afraid to announce that he aimed to provide amusement. In fact, in presenting himself as Locke's disciple, Newbery boldly announced the entertainment-amusement purposes of his books, particularly reflected in his slogan "Trade and Plumb Cake Forever." Nevertheless, the justification for the insertion of amusement in his books was that it combined instruction with morals. As a publisher, Newbery was bound, to a certain extent, to the limits defined by the existing establishment. At the same time, he was quite aware of the inventory of children's literature at the time—chapbooks, lesson books, manuals of good advice, and Aesop's fables—and attempted to use elements of each in order to broaden the appeal of his books as much as possible. His consistent use of chapbook features perhaps reflects, more than anything, the great popularity of chapbooks in his time. Yet, Newbery skillfully combined elements of chapbooks, which appealed to the child, with morality, which appealed to the teacher and parent. An example of this chapbook manipulation is discerned in his first book when he utilizes "Jack the Giant Killer," a characteristic chapbook figure, as a moral preacher. The supposedly entertaining long letter from Jack the Giant Killer to Master Tommy turns out to be a long tiresome lecture on good behavior: "This Character, my Dear, has made every body love you; and, while you continue so good, you may depend on my obliging you with every thing I can. I have here sent you a *Little Pretty Pocket-Book,* which will teach you to play at all those innocent Games that good Boys and Girls divert themselves with" (*A Little Pretty Pocket-Book,* [14–15] 64–65). In another book published by Newbery, *The History of Little Goody Two Shoes* (1765), the heroine Margery, is involved in strange adventures including an accusation of witchcraft (also typical of chapbooks). As Darton claims: "It is plain that the author, in writing this part of the book, had in mind the chapbooks about Fortunatus and Friar Bacon, and, to all appearances, was using the familiar names to make better stuff pass current" (1958, 134). In fact, the story of Margery was a sort of variation of the prohibited tale of Cinderella. It is the story of an unfortunate girl of good family who suffers many trials and tribulations, but eventually marries the heir of the manor and becomes the noble lady of the manor. This sort of story became quite popular and found its way into other children's books, such as Maria Edgeworth's *The Entertaining History of Little Goody Goosecap* (1780), published by John Marshall, or Mary Pilkington's *The Renowned History of Primrose Prettyface, Who By Her Sweetness of Temper and Love of Learning, Was Raised from Being the Daughter of a Poor Cottager, to Great Riches and the Dignity of Lady of the Manor* (1785).

However, the most obvious device Newbery borrowed from chapbooks in order to compete with them was illustrations, which attracted attention and, from that time onward, became an indispensable feature of children's books. As a matter of fact, the use of illustrations in children's books has led to the development of one of the most prominent offshoot phenomena of children's books—the picture book. The picture book is itself responsible for the introduction of an interesting development in children's literature, age stratification. This development has become institutionalized today in children's literature as an elementary and self-evident subsystem. Yet, it was only in the nineteenth century that age differentiation, either in children's literature or in school, was made. During the twentieth century, this stratification has become more refined, as publishers distinguished between young and older children in much more specific divisions (Popular today among publishers are the two-year age divisions, such as 2–4, 6–8, 8–10, etc.).

167

NEWBERY'S AUDIENCE

Newbery's attempt to appeal to parents, educators, and children is already clear from the title and description of his first book. Both were undoubtedly aimed at the middle class and stressed the pedagogical importance of the book, while not losing sight of the fun and amusement: "Little Pretty Pocket-Book Intended for the Instruction and Amusement of Little Master Tommy and Pretty Miss Polly, with Two Letters from Jack the Giant Killer; as also a Ball and Pincushion; The Use of which will infallibly make Tommy a good Boy and Polly a good Girl." Newbery's aim was to appeal to the growing bourgeois audience that had become the main consumer of children's books. This intention is reflected both in the underlying values of the texts as well as in Newbery's marketing devices. The values underlying the texts are discerned for instance in the reward given to virtuous Margery in *The History of Little Goody Two Shoes:*

> Who from a State of Rags and Care,
> And having Shoes but half a Pair
> *Their Fortune and their Fame would fix*
> *and gallop in a Couch for Six.*

(my italics)

His marketing devices, aimed at superseding chapbooks, mainly addressed the bourgeois consumer who could afford to buy his books and deliberately avoided the poor who could not afford them.

COMMERCIAL SUCCESS

It seems clear that Newbery's efforts were fruitful. His first book, *A Little Pretty Pocket-Book* as well as others, were published in several editions between 1744 and the middle of the nineteenth century, despite the fact that he purposely limited himself to a middle- and upper-class children's audience. Apparently, this successful trend carried over to other publishers as well. Toward the end of the eighteenth century, the book market was almost overflooded by publishing for children, as the memories of a German schoolmaster L. F. Gedike, indicate. While visiting the Leipzig Book-Fair in 1707, he wrote:

No other form of literary manufacturing is so active as book-making for young people of all grades and classes. Every Leipzig Summer and Winter Fair throws up a countless number of books of this kind like a flooding tide. And see how young and old rush to buy. . . . They take all kinds of names and forms: almanacks for children, newspapers for children, journals for children, collections for children, stories for children . . . and unlimited variations on the same theme. (Muir 1969, 67)

By the end of the eighteenth century, through constant competition with chapbooks, commercial publishing for children had become an established branch of the publishing field. In this development, Newbery's books had become the model that other commercial publishers sought to immitate.

Religious Publishing for Children

Commercial publishing responded only to the needs of bourgeois society and the upper classes who could afford it; yet there was still a considerable section of the population that knew how to read, but read unsuitable material, at least from the point of view of the religious establishment. As a result, the religious establishment, realizing the dangers lurking in children's reading, began to produce religious tracts that were made available to the poor and were intended as a replacement for chapbooks.

Reading among poor people was a relatively new phenomenon. It was initiated mostly by religious philanthropic endeavors that encouraged the establishment of charity schools where children of the poor could be taught to read. Around the middle of the eighteenth century, the Sunday School Movement, no longer a pioneering organization, had become an institution. Whereas one school was once considered sufficient for an entire district, individual churches now realized the benefits of having a school of their own. The spread of the Sunday school resulted in an enormous growth of the reading public, which meant that the question of reading material was a pertinent one. Moreover, when the establishment discovered what this public was actually reading, the question became even more urgent than ever. The first official Sunday school books were meant to teach reading; they were not intended for home reading. Gradually, however, the religious establishment understood that if children were to be prevented from reading chapbooks hawked by peddlers, they must be provided with appropriate alternative reading matter. Once again, a void in the system occurs that requires filling.

The first person to attempt to satisfy that need was Hanna More (1745–1833). She was among the philanthropists and Sunday school enthusiasts who became alarmed at the impact that unsuitable publications had on the poorer classes (who had learned to read in Sunday schools). The spread of chapbooks was regarded by More as a real danger both to society and to the education of the child. Like others, she believed that the work of the Sunday school would be insufficient without the provision of "safe books"; on this principle, she turned her views into action.

Hanna More was the first to understand that there was a need to produce not only one or two books, but rather to produce a whole literature. It was necessary to replace what she regarded as crude chapbooks, as well as the current political pamphlets that were then consumed by masses of working-class readers. As a result, she urged her evangelical friends at Chapham Common to provide the poor with proper reading material. Aided greatly by their financial support, her efforts proved successful, and in March 1795 the first of the Cheap Repository Tracts was ready. These books, written by More and her friends, aimed at competing with chapbooks by using the familiar format, as well as woodcuts. Another technique used to compete with chapbooks was the serialization of books. Some tracts even deliberately tried to replace chapbooks by offering attractive titles that resembled well-known chapbooks, such as *The Cottage Cook; or, Mrs. Jones' Cheap Dishes*; *Tawny Rachel; or, The Fortune Teller*; *Robert and Richard; or, The Ghost of Poor Molly, Who Was Drowned in Richard's Mill Pond*.

Another tactic used by tract writers to compete with chapbooks was the adoption of familiar chapbook literary genres to didactic teaching. Some prominent forms, like poems (*The Carpenter; or, The Danger of Evil Company*), were intended to replace bawdy ballads, while "Histories" (*Tawny Rachel; or, The Fortune Teller*) were to replace frivolous romances and adventures. Even the sensational and manual books were not exempt. Mother Bunch of the chapbooks, who gave recipes for finding the right husband, was replaced by Mrs. James, who taught "the art of industry and good management." Criminal stories were also used for moral purposes; in religious tracts, crimes were never romanticized (on *Robin Hood*, see Brockman 1982), and criminals were always punished. Even ghosts, the slandered heroes of chapbooks, were used for religious purposes. In *The Deceitfulness of Pleasure*, the appearance of a ghost (the former sinful lady) brings the heroine Catherine back to religious life (cf. Pickering 1981, 104–37). Yet, most interesting of all, was the use of the fairy-tale model by the tracts. Fairy tales posed a more difficult problem than poems or even criminal stories because they were considered the most dangerous reading material for children. Thus, religious tracts could not openly use them; on the other hand, religious educators wanted to take advantage of their popularity and appeal. A solution to this conflict was found in the following manner: fairy tales themselves were never included in tracts, although their literary model was molded into an instructive tale; that is, the fairy was transformed into a religious power, while giants and wild beasts were replaced by dishonesty, gambling, and alcoholism. In *Madge Blarney, the Gypsy Girl* (1797), a poor girl has to fight single-handedly against the wild beasts (the drunken and sinful gypsys); she is eventually saved by religion, which keeps her from falling into sin like her mother (Pickering 1981, 123–26). In this way, the transformed fairy tale of religious tracts was born.

Sometimes tracts even lectured explicitly against chapbooks. In *The Sunday School*, Farmer Hoskins finds out what bawdy songs and stories his daughters have read and makes them promise that they will buy only from "sober honest hawkers" who sold "good little books, Christmas carols and harmless songs" (Pickering 1981, 133). This polemical technique was also practiced by George Mogridge, an evangelical writer, who wrote books that closely resembled the chapbooks. While Mogridge consciously tried to adopt traditional chapbooks as the medium for his own religious and moral teaching, in his books he preached against "idle fictions" and "fleeting joys"; he even condemned "Tom Thumb" as corrupting for children.

In order to compete seriously with chapbooks, it was not enough to try to replace them textually; rather, it was vital to maintain the lowest possible price. This was made possible through generous contributions from religious-oriented societies. For instance, the publication of the Cheap Repository Tracts was backed by Prime Minister William Pitt, the archbishop of Canterbury, and the bishops of Bristol, Bath, Wells, Chester, Durham, Exeter, Ely, Gloucester, London, Lincoln, Salisbury, and Worcester. Consequently, it was possible to sell them at the same price as chapbooks, whose prices ranged from a halfpenny to three halfpennies. Also, distribution of the books was encouraged by offering peddlers and hawkers a favorable discount rate. In this way, the tracts sold over England by the roving venders were able to compete with chapbooks in format, illustrations, price, and distribution. In fact, in the first six weeks of their publication, three hundred thousand tracts were sold, and by March 1796 sales were around two million. Though initially they were intended for *both* children and the poor classes, the lists of 1826 reveal that in that year, there were already books written specifically for children.

Once commercial publishers became aware of the potential of this material, they did not hesitate to use it in their books. These publishers flooded the market with commercially produced books, which, unlike the religious tracts, were not intended for the poor but for the children of the bourgeois and upper classes. Among the most famous was Mrs. Sherwood's *The Fairchild Family* (1818), which became an indispensable item in the library of any well-to-do child.[2]

Thus, out of religious tracts emerged a new model in the children's system—that of the commercially successful religious story probably based on John Janeway's *A Token for Children*.[3] Janeway, and other writers like Mrs. Sherwood and later Sara Trimmer, tried to drive home to children two points: the depravity of their nature and the inevitability of death. Their religious books for children were based on the dogmatic belief that heaven or hell existed at every stage of this mortal life and that conduct on earth leads either to the one or

[2] *The Fairchild Family* was popular even at the beginning of the twentieth century. Frederick Hamilton describes how in 1900 he attended a Fairchild Family dinner where every guest had to appear as one of Mrs. Sherwood's characters (see Avery 1975, 93).

[3] *A Token for Children* opens with the following exhortation to parents: "Are the Souls of your Children of no Value? . . . They are not too little to die, they are not too little to go to Hell, they are not too little to serve their great Master" (Darton 1958, 56).

the other. Authors wrote for the purpose of saving children from hell; accordingly, the child was taught to read for this devout aim. Only when views on education changed with the onset of the moralist school of education, did religious books lose their dominance in the children's system; the new belief in reason demanded something for boys and girls other than harrowing stories of martyrdom and holy deaths. This encouraged books produced primarily by writers of the Rousseauian school.

However, one thing remained the same even when the moralist school had entered the scene; official children's literature, comprising both religious and moralist writing for children, as well as commercial literature, shared a total mistrust of fiction. In 1803, Sara Trimmer revealed a basic mistrust of fairy tales:

> Though we well remember, the interest with which, in our childish days, when books of amusement for children were scarce, we read, or listened to the history of *Little Red Riding Hood* and *Blue Beard*, etc. we do not wish to have such sensations awakened in the hearts of our grandchildren by the same means; for the terrific images which tales of this nature present to the imagination, usually make deep impressions, and injure the tender minds of children, by exciting unreasonable and groundless fears. (Pickering 1981, 43–44)

In *Guardian of Education,* founded in 1809 by Trimmer to defend the young from the dangers of inappropriate literature, she published the following attack on Cinderella (under the initials O.P.): "*Cinderella* is perhaps one of the most exceptional books that was ever written for children. . . . It points some of the worst passions that can enter into the human breast, and of which little children should, if possible, be totally ignorant; such as envy, jealousy, a dislike to mother-in-law and half-sisters, vanity, a love of dress etc., etc." (Darton 1958, 96–97). On another occasion she claimed that Mother Goose was "only fit to fill the heads of children with confused notions of wonderful and supernatural events, brought about by the agency of imaginary beings" (Darton 1958, 97). At the same time that the evangelists thought that imagination was contrary to divine intention (as the imagination of man's heart was intrinsically evil), the Rousseauians believed that reason would inevitably suffer if imagination were cultivated. Even commercial publishers for children adopted these current views on imaginary literature and regarded fairy tales as unsuitable reading material—in spite of their obvious commercial value. However, commercial publishers did try to use the appeal of the fairy tale, although they took special care to announce the virtues of their moralized versions. Thus, E. Newbery published the *Oriental Moralist* (1791) by Richard Johnson (under the pseudonym of the Rev. Mr. Cooper). In the preface, Johnson claimed that he "expunged everything which could give the least offence to the most delicate reader" (Thwaite 1972, 39). His words reflect a deep mistrust by the various establishments of imagination in children's literature, a mistrust so strong that Lamb, at the beginning of the nineteenth century, lamented the absolute absence of the classics he knew as a child. He wrote to Coleridge, "Damn them!—I mean the cursed Barbauld Crew, those Blights and Blasts of all that is Human in man and child," adding that the shelves were piled with Mrs. Barbauld and Mrs. Trimmer nonsense (Townsend 1977, 43).[4]

Officially excluded from all establishment literature for children, fairy tales continued to find refuge in chapbooks, thus reinforcing their negative image. This image persisted until the decline of chapbooks and the simultaneous rehabilitation of fairy tales by official literature in the mid nineteenth century.

Response of the Chapbook to Developments in Children's Literature

Growth in the reading public and competition of official children's literature with the chapbook inevitably forced a change in the production of chapbooks themselves. In order to survive, the publishers of chapbooks had to fight back and react to the new developments. Consequently, two new phenomena arose in popular literature: the growth of chapbook production and the publishing of chapbooks especially for children.

Until the eighteenth century, chapbooks in England were issued chiefly from London, which made their distribution to the other

---

[4] Even in 1887, Charlotte Yonge wrote that she had found village children who were totally ignorant of Cinderella and other imaginative fiction (Avery 1975, 327).

areas quite difficult. By the middle of the eighteenth century, a score of towns in the provinces produced their own chapbooks for large local areas, greatly increasing distribution and sales. Chapmen were no longer dependent upon purchasing books in the capital, but could buy them from a local printer or dealer. However, because of simultaneous developments in publishing for children, chapmen sold not only chapbooks but religious tracts as well. As a result, publishers of chapbooks were forced to compete with those new publications. They did so mainly by publishing chapbooks specifically for children, which even included colored illustrations. These publishers also managed to take advantage of what was prohibited in official children's literature; that is, they published reading material that was available only in chapbook form, such as fairy tales (*Cinderella*), romances (*Tom Hickathrift*), and others written specifically for children (*The House That Jack Built, The Tragical Death of an Apple Pye, Mother Goose,* and many more). Among these publishers of chapbooks for children, the most prominent were Catnach and Dicey. Dicey published between the years 1760 to 1770 some dozens of chapbooks for children, including *The History of Jack and the Giants, The History of Fortunates,* and *The Sleeping Beauty in the Wood.*

James Catnach, who published between 1813 and 1838 quite a few chapbooks for children (such as *Cock Robin, Mother Goose, Simple Simon* and *Tom Hickathrift*) was not only very prolific, but was also the last one to publish chapbooks in the first half of the nineteenth century. Toward the end of the eighteenth century, chapbooks already had begun to decline, mostly because of changes in reading habits, which were influenced by the emergence of newspapers and the success of the novel; as a result, chapbooks gradually faded from popularity. For about forty years, chapbooks scarcely existed in the adult system and eventually were absorbed by the children's system, where they stayed until the middle of the nineteenth century, when they ceased to appear.[5] As Neuburg claims: "Several printers in provincial towns were printing chapbooks for children during the seventeen

---

[5] This is often the case with elements initially belonging to the adult system, then losing their higher status, and finally being accepted by the children's system. The romances, which at first attracted the literate and sophisticated medieval audience (in the original versions), became the stuff of chapbooks shared by children and the poor when they declined. Later, they became the monopoly of children.

eighties and seventeen nineties and continued to do so during the first decades of the 19th century; but the heyday of the chapbooks was over. It was no longer the most important element in popular literature; and it was now entirely intended for child readers" (1968, 65).

This was the process, beginning during the seventeenth century and ending toward the middle of the nineteenth, by which chapbooks were transferred into the system of children's literature.

Chapbooks for children continued to appear as long as they served as the main body of popular literature for children—and as a preserving force of the literature of imagination for children. The new stratification of children's literature into canonized and non-canonized literature was characterized by the opposition of nonimaginary versus imaginary literature, as fairy tales and other imaginary literature was excluded from all forms except chapbooks. Gradually, however, chapbooks for children began to lose their function, as the model of the imaginary story was accepted by the canonized system and as other elements entered into the non-canonized system. Thus stripped of their preserving function and exclusive status, chapbooks for children began to decline. The rise of periodical literature and other cheap publications for children, such as dime novels, serials, and comics, contributed to the decline in demand for chapbooks. Once chapbooks had lost their function of supplying cheap and otherwise inaccessible reading material, they ceased to exist.

Conclusion

This book deals with cultural manipulations. It presents the question of who is culturally responsible for children's literature as a literary product of society. It asks how it is possible to understand the behavior of children's literature as an integral part of culture and why it is so fruitful to do so. It also inquires into children's literature in the broadest possible context—in its multirelations with social norms, literary norms, educational norms—hence suggesting new possibilities to illuminate the field from these angles.

As an answer, it offers the description and analysis of the systemic implications of the status of children's literature in culture. It examines the children's literature as a system in culture, or in other words, as a semiotic phenomenon.

This conceptual framework makes it possible to discuss the functioning of children's literature as a component of cultural systems and to treat cardinal historical (yet dynamic) issues of children's literature in complicated perspectives. It is a motivation for viewing the historical processes and synchronic procedures in broad contexts. Hence issues are discussed on the theoretical and general levels, with the analyzed texts used only as test cases.

In this framework the following questions are raise: Why is children's literature, unlike adult literature, regarded as part of both the educational and the literary systems at one and the same time? What are the implications of this double attribution? How does it affect the development, structure, textual options, readers and writers of children's literature? How and to what extent do notions of childhood determine the character of the texts for the child on the level of poetic norms, as well as in regard to the acceptance of the texts by the "people of culture"? Furthermore, it asks how writers for children react to such societal and poetic demands in producing their texts.

While examining these processes and procedures it becomes clear that they are neither random nor static. Rather they are described as accountable and dynamic processes, governing the history and the development of children's literature since its inception.

Indeed, the book opens with: "In the beginning was the Logos." It starts by pursuing the linkage between the creation of the notion of childhood and the texts for the child. Following Ariès's famous thesis, the book describes one of the results of the emergence of the notion of childhood—the appearance of books for the child, the emergence of children's literature. This historical process is described here from various aspects: the changing ideas of childhood resulting in different texts for the child, especially in regard to the child as implied reader, with "Little Red Riding Hood" serving as a test case; the dependence of children's literature on the educational system as it affected both its own development and its model of development, which turn out to be the same in different national children's literatures (Hebrew children's literature serves as a test case). On the other hand, one of the results of the new system of education was the emergence of a new readership, which in its search for reading material became an enthusiastic promoter of chapbooks, the non-canonized literature of the time.

How then was canonized children's literature forced to react to the reading of material by children that was regarded as "unfit," "trash literature"? The emergence of children's literature out of the non-canonized adult system is described in the book in terms of the stratification of the system. The stratification led to the creation of a new opposition within the literary system: the opposition between children's literature and adult literature. In such a way, every stage in the development of children's literature is described not only in terms of its linkage to the educational system, but in terms of its relations with the entire literary polysystem, including the need to compete with non-canonized adult literature.

As the book's point of departure is the double systemic attribution of children's literature, it examines this attribution in both the historical context and the actual implications of writing for children. Undoubtedly this attribution can account for the inferior status of children's literature in culture in general, and in the literary polysystem in particular. This inferior status implies that writing for children deprives the writer of all status symbols acquired by writers for adults. The writer for children not only suffers from a culturally inferior status, but he is subject to more compulsory poetic constraints than the writer for adults. These constraints must be obeyed by writers for children if they wish to ensure their acceptance by the establishment of children's literature.

The issue of poetic constraints is analyzed in the book with regard to the establishment's requirements as well as to the poetic and thematic implications (*Danny the Champion of the World* serves as a test case). The question of poetic constraints that result from the systemic position of children's literature is further discussed from an additional point of view—that of translation of children's books. The discussion of translation is mainly devoted to translation of literary models involving the transfer from the adult to the children's system (*Robinson Crusoe* and *Gulliver's Travels* serve as test cases). In order to overcome both the inferior status and the poetic constraints, writers are led to seek various solutions. In this context the book examines two such solutions found at the two opposite extremes: ambivalent texts and non-canonized literature for children.

Analysis of the first solution, that of the ambivalent text, reveals that writers overcome systemic constraints by manipulating two addressees and the current literary models. They use the child as a pseudo-addressee but actually assume the adult as a reader, hence gaining the liberty to manipulate the existing models of children's literature and to suggest a new model (*Alice in Wonderland* serves as a test case).

In examining the other opposite solution, that of non-canonized children's literature, it is maintained that writers manage to ignore constraints by consciously waiving adult approval. This is textually done by creating a world that excludes adults, creating the illusion of an exclusive world of children (the Nancy Drew series and Enid Blyton's books serve as test cases).

This book examines the need for children's literature to function while "walking the tightrope" between the official addressee (the child) and those who decide the character of his culture (the adults). In this context it explores the interrelations between literary and social constraints that create the history, inventory, and structure of children's literature. How children's literature manages to function in such a complicated net of systems is actually the core of the book; it is practically what it is all about.

This however is just the beginning. I hope that the directions and questions suggested by my book will prompt further research and study in children's literature.

Bibliography

Altick, Richard D. 1957. *The English Common Reader.* Chicago: University of Chicago Press.

Arbuthnot, May Hill, and Zena Sutherland. 1972. *Children and Books.* Chicago: Scott, Foresman.

Ariès, Philippe. 1962. *Centuries of Childhood.* London: Jonathan Cape.

——— . 1972. "At the Point of Origin." In Brooks 1972, 15–23.

Arnold, Klaus. 1980. *Kind und Gesellschaft in Mittelalter und Renaissance.* Würzburg: Ferdinand Schoningh.

Ashton, John. 1882. *Chapbooks of the Eighteenth Century.* London: Chatto and Windus.

Avery, Gillian. 1971. "Fairy Tales with a Purpose." In Gray 1971, 321–25.

———. 1975. *Childhood's Pattern.* London: Hodder and Stoughton.

Avery, Gillian, with Angela Bull. 1965. *Nineteenth-Century Children: Heroes and Heroines in English Children's Stories, 1780–1900.* London: Hodder and Stoughton.

Avery, Gillian, Lea Alec, Joan R. Robinson, and Roy Brown. 1971. "Writing for Children: A Social Engagement?" *Children's Literature in Education* 2:17–29.

Azaaola, Professor José Miguel de, President of the Jury. 29 September 1962. Speech delivered for the Hans Christian Andersen Award, Hamburg. International Youth Library, Hektograph no. 697.

Baran, H., ed. 1976. *Semiotics and Structuralism.* New York: Art and Science Press, White Plains.

Barry, Florence V. 1922. *A Century of Children's Books.* London: Methuen and Co.; reissued 1968, Singing Tree Press.

Bashevis-Singer, Isaac. 1977. "Isaac Bashevis-Singer on Writing for Children." *Children's Literature* 6:9–16.

Bawden, Nina. 1974. "A Dead Pig and My Father." *Children's Literature in Education* 5:3–13.

Benesch, Kurt. 1968. "Jugendbuch—Literatur oder nicht?" *Jugend und Buch* 17:3–6.

Bennett, H. S. 1969. *English Books and Readers.* Cambridge: Cambridge University Press.

Ben-Porat, Ziva. 1978. "Reader, Text and Literary Allusion: Aspects in the

Actualization of Literary Allusions." *Ha-sifrut* 26:1–26. In Hebrew, English summary, i–iv.

———. 1979. "Method in Madness: Notes on the Structure of Parody Based on Mad TV Satires." *Poetics Today* 1:245–72.

Bettelheim, Bruno. 1976. *The Uses of Enchantment.* New York: Knopf.

Biegel, Paul. 1975. "Report of the Jury Awarding the State Prize." *The Junior Bookshelf* 39:9–11.

Binder, Lucia. 1977. "Hans Christian Andersen Prizes 1976." In *How Can Children's Literature Meet the Needs of Modern Children: Fairy-Tale and Poetry Today.* Fifteenth IBBy Congress, Arbeitkreis für Jugendliteratur, Munich, 123–27.

———. 1978. "Hans Christian Andersen Prizes 1978." In *Modern Realistic Stories for Children and Young People.* Sixteenth IBBy Congress, Arbeitkreis für Jugendliteratur, Munich.

Bishen, Edward, ed. 1975. *The Thorny Paradise.* London: Kestrel Books.

Black, Kathleen. 1977. "The Sea Dream: Peter Pan and Treasure Island." *Children's Literature* 6:165–81.

Boas, George. 1969. *The Cult of Childhood.* London: Warburg Institute, University of London.

Bolte, Johannes, and George Polívka. 1963. *Anmerkungen zu den Kinder und Hausmärchen der Brüder Grimm.* 5 vols. Hildesheim: George Olms Verlagsbuchhandlung.

Bowen, Naomi. 1975. "Gillian Avery: A Conversation." *School Librarian* 23:205–8.

Bravo-Villasante, Carmen. 1977. *Weltgeschichte der Kinder und Jugendliteratur.* Hannover: Schroedel Verlag.

Briggs, Katherine M. [1967] 1977. *The Fairies.* London: Routledge and Kegan Paul.

———. 1977. *A Dictionary of Fairies.* London: Penguin.

Brinsmead, H. R. 1969. "How and Why I Write for Young People." *Journal of the School Library* 2:4.

Brockman, Bennett H. 1982. "Robin Hood and the Invention of Children's Literature." *Children's Literature* 10:1–17.

Brooks, Peter, ed. [1969] 1972. *The Child's Part.* Boston: Beacon Press.

Brüder Grimm. 1980. *Kinder und Hausmärchen,* ed. Heinz Rölleke. Stuttgart: Reclam.

Butler, Francelia. 1976. "Skip Rope Rhymes as a Reflection of American Culture." *Children's Literature* 5:104–16.

———. 1977. "Between 1776 and 1976." *Children's Literature* 6:61–76.

Campe, Joachim Heinrich. [1860] 1978. *Robinson der Jüngere.* Dortmund: Harenberg, Die bibliophilen Tachenbücher.

Carroll, Lewis. [1887] 1961. "Alice on the Stage." In Collingwood 1961, 163–74.

———. [1932] 1971. *The Rectory Umbrella.* New York: Dover.

Chambers, Aidan. 1969. *The Reluctant Reader.* Oxford: Pergamon Press.

———. 1977. "The Reader in the Book." *Signal* 8:23, 64–87.

Chambers, Dewey W. 1971. *Children's Literature in the Curriculum.* Chicago: Rand McNally.

Charvat, William. 1968a. *The Profession of Authorship in America, 1800–1870.* Columbus: Ohio State University Press.

———. 1968b. "Literary Economics and Literary History." In *Charvat* 1968a, 283–97.

Chauncy, Nan. 1968. "Why Write for Children?" *Journal of the School Library Association,* North Queensland, 1:3–4, 5–8.

Collingwood, Stuart Dodgson. 1898. *The Life and Letters of Lewis Carroll.* London: T. Fisher.

———. [1899] 1961. *The Unknown Lewis Carroll.* Published under the title *The Lewis Carroll Picture Book.* New York: Dover.

Collinson, Roger. 1973. "The Children's Author and His Readers." *Children's Literature in Education* 4:10, 37–49.

Cott, Jonathan, ed. 1978. *Beyond the Looking Glass.* New York: Wallaby Pocket Book.

Coveney, Peter. 1967. *The Image of Childhood.* London: Penguin, Peregrine Books.

Crews, Frederick. 1963. *The Pooh Perplex.* New York: Dutton.

Cripps, Elizabeth A. 1983. "'Alice' and Reviewers." *Children's Literature* 11:32–48.

Darling, Richard. 1968. *The Rise of Children's Book Reviewing in America, 1865–1881.* New York: R. R. Bowker.

Darnton, Robert. 1984. *The Great Cat Massacre.* New York: Basic Books.

Darton, Harvey F. J. 1958. *Children's Books in England.* Cambridge: Cambridge University Press.

Davenport, Tom. 1981. "Some Personal Notes on Adapting Folk-Fairy Tales to Film." *Children's Literature* 9:107–15.

Davis, James E. 1976. "Recent Censorship Fires: Flareups or Holocaust?" *Journal of Research and Development in Education* 9:22–32.

Delarue, Paul. 1957. *Le Conte populaire francais.* Paris: Editions Erasme.

deMause, Lloyd, ed. 1975. *The History of Childhood.* New York: Harper and Row, Harper Torchbooks.

Dickinson, Peter. [1970] 1976. "A Defence of Rubbish." In Fox et al. 1976, 73–76.

Dinges, Ottilie. 1979. "Vorschulische literarische Erziehung." In *Lexikon der Kinder und Jugendliteratur,* 730–51. Weinheim and Basel: Beltz.

Doderer, Klaus, ed. 1981. *Ästhetick der Kinderliteratur.* Weinheim and Basel: Beltz.

Dohm, Janice H. 1957. "Newbery and Carnegie Awards." *Junior Bookshelf* 21:5–15.

Donelson, Ken. 1975. "Censorship and Arizona English Teaching, 1971–1974." *Arizona English Bulletin* 17:1–39.

———. 1978. "Nancy, Tom and Assorted Friends." *Children's Literature* 7:17–44.

Dyhrenfurth, Irene. 1967. *Geschichte des deutschen Jugendbuches.* Zürich and Freiburg: Atlantis Verlag.

Egoff, Sheila, G. T. Stubbs, and F. Ashley. 1969. *Only Connect.* New York: Oxford University Press.

Eliav, Mordechai. 1960. *Jewish Education in Germany in the Period of Enlightenment and Emancipation.* Jerusalem: Hasochnut Hayehudit. In Hebrew.

Ellis, Alec. 1968. *How to Find Out About Children's Literature?* London: Pergamon Press.

Elschenbroich, Donata. 1977. *Kinder werden nicht geboren.* Frankfurt and Munich: Päd Extra.

Erlich, Victor. [1955] 1969. *Russian Formalism.* The Hague: Mouton.

Escarpit, Robert. [1958] 1968a. *La sociologie de la littérature.* Paris: PUF.

———. 1968b. "The Sociology of Literature." In *The International Encyclopedia of the Social Sciences,* vol. 9, 417–85. New York: MacMillan.

Esmonde, Margaret P., and Priscilla A. Ord. eds. 1979. *Proceedings of the Fifth Annual Conference of the Children's Literature Association,* Harvard University, March 1978. Villanova: Villanova University Press.

Even-Zohar, Itamar. 1974. "Israeli Hebrew Literature: A Historical Model." English version in Even-Zohar 1978a, 75–92.

———. 1975. "Decisions in Translating Poetry." *Ha-sifrut* 21:32–45. In Hebrew.

———. 1978a. *Papers in Historical Poetics.* Tel Aviv: Porter Institute for Poetics and Semiotics, Tel Aviv University Press.

———. [1974] 1978b. "The Relations Between Primary and Secondary Systems Within the Literary Polysystem." In Even-Zohar 1978a, 14–20.

———. 1978c. "Universals of Literary Contacts." In Even-Zohar 1978a, 45–54.

———. 1978d. "The Position of Translated Literature Within the Literary Polysystem." In Even-Zohar 1978a, 21–27.

———. 1978e. "Israeli Hebrew Literature—A Historical Model." In Even-Zohar 1978a, 75–94.

———. 1978f. "Interference in Dependent Literary Polysystems." In Even-Zohar 1978a, 54–62.

———. 1978g. "Russian and Hebrew: The Case of Dependent Poly-systems." In Even-Zohar 1978a, 63–74.

———. 1979. "Polysystem Theory." *Poetics Today* 1:287–310.

———. 1981. "Translation Theory Today." *Poetics Today* 2:1–7.

Ewers, Hans-Heino, ed. 1980. *Kinder und Jugendliteratur der Aufklärung.* Stuttgart: Reclam.

Fadiman, Clifton. 1976. "The Case for a Children's Literature." *Children's Literature* 5:9–21.

Fenwick, S. I., ed. 1967. *A Critical Approach to Children's Literature.* Chicago: University of Chicago Press.

Fischer, Margery. 1966. "Acceptance Speech." *Children's Book News* 6:163–64.

Flescher, Jacqueline. 1969. "The Language of Nonsense in *Alice.*" In Brooks 1969, 128–44.

Fox, Geoff, et al., eds. 1976. *Writers, Critics and Children.* London: Heine-mann Educational Books.

Freeman, James A. 1977. "Donald Duck: How Children (Mainly Boys) Viewed Their Parents (Mainly Fathers), 1943–1960." *Children's Literature* 6:150–63.

Freudmann, Felix R. 1963. "Realism and Magic in Perrault's Fairy-Tales." *L'Esprit Créateur* 3:116–22.

Gans, H. J. 1975. *Popular Culture and High Culture.* New York: Basic Books.

Gardam, Jane. 1978. "On Writing for Children: Some Wasps in the Mar-malade." Part 1. *Horn Book Magazine* 60:489–96.

Gardner, Martin. [1965] 1969. "A Child's Garden of Bewilderment." In Egoff et al. 1969, 150–55.

———, ed. 1977. *The Annotated Alice.* London: Penguin.

Garfield, Leon. 1970. "Writing for Children." *Children's Literature in Educa-tion* 1:56–63.

Gattégno, Jean. 1977. *Lewis Carroll.* Translated by Rosemary Sheed. Lon-don: George Aleen and Unwin.

Gavalt, Paul, ed. 1931. *Les livres de l'enfance du XVe au XIXe siècle.* Paris: Gumuchian and Cie.

Gerhardt, Lillian N. 1973. *Issues in Children's Book Selection.* New York: R. R. Bowker.

Girouard, Mark. 1978. *Life in the English Country House.* New Haven: Yale University Press.

Göbles Hubert, ed. 1980. *Hundert alte Kinderbücher aus Barock und Aufklärung.* Dortmund: Harenberg, Die Bibliophilen Taschenbücher.

Goffman, Irving. 1959. *The Presentation of Self in Everyday Life.* New York: Doubleday.

185

Gray, Donald. 1971. *Alice in Wonderland.* New York: Norton.

Green, Lancelyn Roger. 1946. *Andrew Lang—A Critical Biography.* Leicester: Edmund Ward.

———. 1949. *The Story of Lewis Carroll.* London: Methuen and Co.

———. 1960. *Lewis Carroll.* London: Bodley Head.

———. [1962] 1969a. "The Golden Age of Children's Books." In Egoff et al. 1969, 1–16.

———. 1969b. *Tellers of Tales.* Revised edition. London: Kaye and Ward.

Hagen, Rolf. 1955. "Perraults Märchen und die Brüder Grimm." *Zeitschrift für Deutsche Philologie* 74:392–410.

Hallays, André. 1926. *Les Perrault.* Paris: Perrin.

Hanks, Carole, and D. T. Hanks, Jr. 1978. "Perrault's 'Little Red Riding Hood': Victim of the Revisers." *Children's Literature* 7:68–77.

Härtling, Peter. 1977. "Über die Schwierigkeiten und das Vergütungen bei Schreiben für Kinder." *Jugend und Buch* 26:1–4.

Haviland, Virginia. 1966. *A Guide to Reference Sources.* Washington, D.C.: Library of Congress.

———. 1974. *Children and Literature.* London: Bodley Head.

Hazard, Paul. 1947. *Books, Children and Men.* Translated by Marguerite Mitchell. Boston: Horn Book.

Heisig, James W. 1977. "Bruno Bettelheim and the Fairy-Tales." *Children's Literature* 6:93–114.

Helson, Ravenna. 1974. "The Psychological Origins of Fantasy for Children in Mid-Victorian England." *Children's Literature* 3:66–76.

———. 1976. "Change, Tradition and Critical Styles in the Contemporary World of Children's Books." *Children's Literature* 5:22–39.

Holmes, James S., et al., eds. 1978. *Literature and Translation: New Perspectives in Literary Studies.* Leuven: Acco.

Hrushovski, Benjamin. 1974. "Principles of a Unified Theory of the Literary Text." In Ziva Ben-Porat and Benjamin Hrushovski, *Structuralist Poetics in Israel.* Department of Poetics and Comparative Literature, Tel Aviv University, 13–23.

———. 1979. "The Structure of Semiotic Objects: A Three-Dimensional Model." *Poetics Today* 1:363–76.

Hudson, Derek. 1978. *Lewis Carroll: An Illustrated Biography.* New York: New American Library.

Hughes, Felicity A. 1978. "Children's Literature: Theory and Practice." *ELH* 45:542–61.

Hunter, Mollie. 1975. *Talent Is Not Enough.* New York: Harper and Row.

Hürlimann, Bettina. 1967. *Three Centuries of Children's Books in Europe.* Translated and edited by B. W. Alderson. London: Oxford University Press.

Iser, Wolfgang. 1974. *The Implied Reader*. Baltimore: Johns Hopkins University Press.

Jakobson, Roman. 1959. "On Linguistic Aspects of Translation." In Reuben A. Brower, ed. 1959. *On Translation*. New York: Oxford University Press, 232–39.

———. 1960. "Concluding Statement: Linguistics and Poetics." In T. A. Sebeok, ed. 1960. *Style in Language*. Cambridge, Mass.: MIT Press, 350–77.

———. 1971. "The Dominant." In Matejka and Pomorska 1971, 82–87.

Jambeck, Thomas. 1974. "Chaucer's Treatise on the Astrolabe." *Children's Literature* 3:117–22.

James, Higgins E. 1977. *Beyond Words*. New York: Teachers College Press, Columbia University.

Jan, Isabelle. 1969. "Children's Literature and Bourgeois Society Since 1860." In Brooks 1969, 57–72.

———. 1973. *On Children's Literature*. Translated from the French with a preface by Catherine Storr. London: Allen Lane.

Jauss, Hans R. 1970. "Literary History as Challenge to Literary Theory." *New Literary History* 2:7–37.

Johansen, Erna M. 1978. *Betrogene Kinder. Eine Sozialgeschichte der Kindheit*. Frankfurt: Fischer Taschenbuch Verlag.

Kanfer, Stefan. 1980. "A Lovely, Profitable World of Kid Lit." *Time*, 29 December 1980, 38–41.

Kanipe, Esther S. 1969. "Hetzel and the Bibliothèque d'Éducation." In Brooks 1969, 73–85.

Kiefer, Monica M. 1948. *American Children Through Their Books, 1700–1835*. Philadelphia: University of Pennsylvania Press.

Klingberg, Göte, Mary Ørvig, and Amor Stuart, eds. 1978. *Children's Books in Translation: The Situation and the Problems*. Proceedings of the Third Symposium of the International Research Society for Children's Literature. Stockholm: Almqvist and Wiksell Int.

Koppes, Phyllis Bixler. 1978. "Tradition and the Individual Talent of Frances Hodgson Burnett." *Children's Literature* 7:191–207.

Krampen, Martin. 1980. " 'Developmental Semiotics' and Children's Drawing." *Versus* 25:87–100.

Kreuzer, Helmut. 1967. "Trivialliteratur als Forschungsproblem: Zur Kritik des deutschen Trivialromans seit der Aufklärung." *DVjs* 41:173–91.

Kuhn, Thomas. 1962. *The Structure of Scientific Revolutions*. Chicago: University of Chicago Press.

Lanes, Selma G. 1971. *Down the Rabbit-Hole: Adventures and Misadventures in the Realm of Children's Literature*. New York: Atheneum.

Leavis, Q. D. [1932] 1979. *Fiction and the Reading Public*. London: Penguin, Peregrine Books.

Leeson, Robert. 1976. "What Were We Arguing About?" *Signal* 7:20.

Lennon, Florence Becker. 1962. *The Life of Lewis Carroll.* New York: Collier Books.

Lewis, C. S. [1952] 1969. "On Three Ways of Writing for Children." In Egoff et al. 1969, 207–20.

Lexikon der Kinder und Jugendliteratur. 1975–1979. Edited by Klaus Doderer. 3 vols. Weinheim and Basel: Beltz.

Lindgren, Astrid. 1978. "A Small Chat with a Future Children's Book Author." *Bookbird* 16:9–12.

Lotman, Jurij. 1973. *Structure du texte artistique.* Paris: Gallimard.

———. 1976a. "The Content and Structures of the Concept of 'Literature.'" *PTL* 2:339–56.

———. 1976b. "Culture and Information." *Disposito* 1:213–15.

———. [1974] 1977. "The Dynamic Model of Semiotic Systems." *Semiotica* 21:193–210.

Lotman, Jurij, et al. 1975. "Theses on the Semiotic Study of Cultures." In Sebeok 1975, 57–84.

Lukens, Rebecca. 1976. *A Critical Handbook of Children's Literature.* Illinois: Scott Foresman and Co.

———. 1978. "The Child, the Critic and a Good Book." *Language Arts* 55:452–54, 546.

Lüthi, Max. 1976. *Once Upon a Time.* Translated by Lee Chadeayne and Paul Gottwald. Bloomington: Indiana University Press.

MacCann, Donnarae. [1965] 1969. "Wells of Fancy, 1865–1965." In Egoff et al. 1969, 133–49.

McDowell, Myles. 1976. "Fiction for Children and Adults: Some Essential Differences." In Fox et al. 1976, 140–56.

Macleod, Anne Scott. 1975. *A Moral Tale.* Hamden, Conn.: Archon Books.

———. 1976. "For the Good of the Country." *Children's Literature* 5:40–51.

McMunn, William, Robert Barstow, Allen M. Riggio, Milla B. McMunn, Meredith Tilbury, and Bennett A. Brockman. 1975. "A Symposium on Children and Literature in the Middle Ages.: *Children's Literature* 4: 36–63.

Matejka, Ladislav, ed. 1976. *Sound, Sign and Meaning: Quinquagenary of the Prague Linguistic Circle.* Michigan Slavic Contributions, no. 6. Ann Arbor: Slavic Department, University of Michigan.

Matejka, Ladislav, and Krystyna Pomorska, eds. 1971. *Readings in Russian Poetics.* Cambridge, Mass.: MIT Press.

Matejka, Ladislav, and Irwin R. Titunik, eds. 1976. *Semiotics of Art.* Cambridge, Mass.: MIT Press.

Meigs, Cornelia, et al., eds. 1969. *A Critical History of Children's Literature.* New York: Macmillan.

Michaelis-Jena, Ruth. 1970. *The Brothers Grimm*. London: Routledge and Kegan Paul.

Molson, Francis. 1977. "Portraits of the Young Writer in Children's Fiction." *Lion and the Unicorn* 1:70–90.

Moore, Rosa Anne. 1975. "Laura Ingalls Wilder's Orange Notebooks and the Art of Little House Books." *Children's Literature* 4:105–19.

————. 1978. "The Little House Books: Rose-Colored Classics." *Children's Literature* 7:7–16.

Moses, Montrose J. 1907. *Children's Books and Reading*. New York: Mitchell Kennerly; republished 1971, Ann Arbor, Mich.: Gryphon Books.

Muir, Percy H. 1969. *English Children's Books*. New York: Fredrick A. Frager.

Mukařovský, Jan. [1936] 1970. *Aesthetic Function, Norm and Values as Social Facts*. Translated by Mark E. Suino. Ann Arbor: University of Michigan Press.

Neuburg, Victor E. 1968. *The Penny Histories*. London: Oxford University Press.

————. 1969. "The Diceys and the Chapbook Trade." *Library* 24:219–31.

————. 1972. *Chapbooks: A Guide to Reference Material*. London: Woburn Press.

————. 1977. *Popular Literature*. London: Penguin.

Neuschäfer, Hans-Jörg. 1971. "Mit Rücksicht auf das Publikum . . . : Probleme der Kommunikation und Herstellung von Konsens in der Unterhaltungsliteratur, dargestellt am Beispiel der Kameliendame." *Poetica* 4:478–514.

Newbery, John. [1767] 1966. *A Little Pretty Pocket-Book*. A facsimile, with an introductory essay and bibliography by M. F. Thwaite. Oxford: Oxford University Press.

Nodelman, Perry. 1978. "Little Red Riding Hood Rides Again and Again and Again and Again." *Proceedings of the Fifth Annual Conference of the Children's Literature Association*, Harvard University, 70–77.

Ofek, Uriel. 1979. *Hebrew Children's Literature: The Beginnings*. Tel Aviv: Porter Institute for Poetics and Semiotics. In Hebrew.

Opie, Peter, and Iona Opie. 1974. *The Classic Fairy-Tales*. London: Oxford University Press.

————. 1980. "One Shilling Plain, Eighteeen-Pence Coloured." *TLS*, 1030.

Patterson, Sylvia. 1971. *Rousseau's Émile and Early Children's Literature*. New York: Scarecrow.

Pavel, Thomas G. 1976. " 'Possible World' in Literary Semantics." *Journal of Aesthetics and Art Criticism* 34:165–76.

Pellowski, Anne. 1968. *The World of Children's Literature*. New York: R. R. Bowker.

Perrault, Charles. 1967. *Contes.* Textes établis avec introduction, sommaire biographique, bibliographie, notices, etc. par Gilbert Rouger. Paris: Garnier.

Perrin, Noel. 1969. *Dr. Bowdler's Legacy: A History of Expurgate Books in England and America.* New York: Atheneum.

Perry, Menakhem. 1979. "Literary Dynamics: How the Order of a Text Creates Its Meaning." *Poetics Today* 1:35–64, 311–61.

———. 1979. "Alternative Patterning. Mutually Exclusive Sign-Sets in Literary Texts." *Versus* 24:83–106.

———. 1985. "The Combined Discourse—Several Remarks About the Definition of the Phenomenon." *Poetics Today,* in press.

Perry, Menakhem, and Meir Sternberg. 1968. "The King Through Ironic Eyes: The Narrator's Devices in the Biblical Story of David and Bathsheba and Two Excursuses on the Theory of the Narrative Text." *Ha-sifrut* 1:263–92. In Hebrew, English summary, ii–v.

Peyton, Kathleen. 1970. "The Carnegie Medal Speech of Acceptance." *Junior Bookshelf* 34:269–71.

Phillips, Robert, ed. 1971. *Aspects of Alice.* New York: Vintage Books.

Pickering, Samuel F., Jr. 1977. "The Evolution of Genre: Fictional Biographies for Children in the Eighteenth Century." *Journal of Narrative Technique* 7:1–23.

———. 1981. *John Locke and Children's Books in Eighteenth-Century England.* Knoxville: University of Tennessee Press.

Pierpont Morgan Library. 1975. *Early Children's Books and Their Illustrations.* Toronto: Oxford University Press.

Pinchbeck, Ivy, and Margaret Hewitt. 1973. *Children in English Society.* 2 vols. London: Routledge and Kegan Paul.

Plessen, Marie Louise, and Peter von Zahn. 1979. *Zwei Jahrtausende Kindheit.* Cologne: VGS.

Pollock, Linda A. 1983. *Forgotten Children.* Cambridge: Cambridge University Press.

Racist and Sexist Images in Children's Books. 1975. London: Writers and Readers Publishing Cooperative.

Ray, Sheila G. 1974. *Children's Fiction.* Leicester: Brockhampton Press.

Robert, Marthe, 1969. "The Grimm Brothers." *Yale French Studies* 43:44–57.

Rölleke, Heinz. 1975. *Die älteste Marchensammlung der Brüder Grimm.* Cologne and Geneva: Bibliotheca Bodmeriana.

Rosenbach, A. S. W. [1966]. 1971. *Early American Children's Books.* New York: Dover.

Rosenthal, Lynne. 1974. "Misunderstood: A Victorian Children's Book for Adults." *Children's Literature* 3:94–102.

Saxby, H. M. 1969. *A History of Australian Children's Literature*. 2 vols. Sydney: Wentworth Books.

Scherf, Walter. 1969. "Book Awards and Some Insight to Be Gained from Them." In *Preisgekrönte Kinderbücher*. Munich, Pullach, and Berlin: Verlag Docume Dokumentation, vii–ix.

Sebeok, Thomas A., ed. 1975. *The Tell-Tale Sign: A Survey of Semiotics Texts*. Lisse: Peter de Ridder Press.

Shavit, Zohar. [1978] 1982. *The Literary Life in Eretz-Israel*. Tel Aviv: Porter Institute for Poetics and Semiotics in Collaboration with Hakibutz-Hameuchad.

———. 1980–81. "The Ambivalent Status of Texts: A Rejoinder." *Poetics Today* 2:199–202.

Shmeruk, Khone. 1978. *Yiddish Literature: Aspects of its History*. Tel Aviv: Porter Institute for Poetics and Semiotics, Tel Aviv University. In Hebrew.

Shukman, Ann. 1977. *Literature and Semiotics: A Study of the Writings of Yu M. Lotman*. Amsterdam: North Holland.

Sloane, William. 1955. *Children's Books in England and in America in the Seventeenth Century*. New York: Columbia University Press.

Smith, Barbara Herrnstein. 1968. *Poetic Closure*. Chicago: University of Chicago Press.

Smith, James Steel. 1967. *A Critical Approach to Children's Literature*. New York: McGraw Hill.

Smith, Lillian H. 1970. *The Unreluctant Years*. Chicago: American Library Association.

Soriano, Marc. 1969. "From Tales of Warning to Formulettes: The Oral Tradition in French Children's Literature." In Brooks 1969, 4–43.

———. 1978. *Les Contes de Perrault*. Paris: Gallimard.

Southhall, Ivan. 1975. *A Journey of Discovery: On Writing for Children*. Harmondsworth, Middlesex: Kestrel Books.

Steig, Michael. 1980–81. "The Ambivalent Status of Texts: Some Comments." *Poetics Today* 2:193–98.

Stein, Ruth M. 1976. "Confronting Censorship in the Elementary Schools." *Journal of Research and Development in Education* 9:41–51.

Stewart, Susan. 1979. *Nonsense*. Baltimore: Johns Hopkins University Press.

Stone, Harry. 1977–80. "Dickens, Cruikshank and Fairy-Tales." *Princeton University Library Chronicle* 35:213–47.

Stoney, Barbara. 1974. *Enid Blyton: A Biography*. London: Hodder.

Sutherland, Robert. 1970. *Language and Lewis Carroll*. The Hague: Mouton.

Sutton-Smith, Brian. 1981. "Early Stories as Poetry." *Children's Literature* 9:137–50.

Thwaite, Mary F. 1972. *From Primer to Pleasure*. London: Library Association.

Toury, Gideon. 1974. "Literature as a Polysystem." *Ha-sifrut* 18–19:1–19. In Hebrew.

———. 1977. *Translational Norms and Literary Translation into Hebrew: 1935–1940.* Tel Aviv: Porter Institute for Poetics and Semiotics. In Hebrew.

———. 1980a. "Translated Literature—System, Norm, Performance: Toward a TT-Oriented Approach to Literary Translation." *Poetics Today* 2:9–28.

———. 1980b. *In Search of a Theory of Translation.* Tel Aviv: Porter Institute for Poetics and Semiotics.

Townsend, John Rowe. 1971. *A Sense of Story.* London: Longman.

———. 1977. *Written for Children.* London: Penguin.

———. 1979. *A Sounding of Story Tellers.* Harmondsworth, Middlesex: Kestrel Books.

Travaux, Tartu. 1976. *Travaux sur les systèmes de signes: École de Tartu.* Brussels: Complexe.

Travers, Pamela. 1975. "On Not Writing for Children." *Children's Literature* 5:15–22.

Trigon, Jean de. 1950. *Histoire de la littérature enfantine.* Paris: Hachette.

Tucker, Nicholas. 1976. *Suitable for Children?* Sussex: Sussex University Press.

Tuer, A. W. 1897. *The History of the Hornbook.* London: Leadenhall Press.

———. [1899] 1969. *Stories from Old-Fashioned Children's Books.* New York: Augustus M. Kelley.

Tynjanov, Jurij. [1929] 1971. "On Literary Evaluation." In Matejka and Pomorska 1971, 66–78.

Tynjanov, Jurij, and Roman Jakobson. [1929] 1971. "Problems in the Study of Literature and Language." In Matejka and Pomorska 1971, 79–81.

Velten, H. U. 1930. "The Influence of Charles Perrault's *Contes de ma mere l'oie* on German folktale." *Germanic Review* 5:4–18.

Vinogradov, Victor. 1922. "Sjužet i kompozicija povesti Gogolja 'Nos.'" *Načala,* 82–105. Hebrew translation in *Ha-sifrut* 1:308–18.

Vodička, Felix. [1942] 1976. "Response to Verbal Art." In Matejka and Titunik 1976, 197–208.

Voloshinov, V. N. [1929] 1973. *Marxism and Philosophy of Language.* Translated by Ladislav Matejka and I. R. Titunik. New York: Seminar Press.

Walsh, Jill Paton. 1973. "The Writer's Responsibility." *Children's Literature in Education* 4:30–36.

Watson, George, ed. 1971. *The New Cambridge Bibliography for English Literature.* Vol. 2, 1660–1800. Cambridge: Cambridge University Press.

Webb, Kaye. 1970. "Ten Years Later." *Books, Journal of the National Book League* 2:3–4.

Weber-Kellermann, Ingeborg. 1979. *Die Kindheit: Eine Kulturgeschichte.* Frankfurt and Munich: Insel Verlag.

Welch, d'Alté. 1972. *A Bibliography of American Children's Books Published Prior to 1821.* Worcester, Mass: American Antiquarian Society.

Whitehead, Frank, A. C. Capey, Wendy Moddren, and Alan Wellings. 1978. *Children and Their Books.* London: School Council Publication, Macmillan Education.

Wienold, Götz. 1981. "Some Basic Aspects of Text Processing." *Poetics Today* 2:97–109.

Wood, James Playsted. 1966. *The Snark Was a Boojum.* New York: Pantheon Books.

Wright, Louis Boker. 1963. *Middle-Class Culture in Elizabethan England.* New York: Cornell University Press.

Wunderlich, Richard, and Thomas J. Morrissey. 1982. "The Desecration of 'Pinocchio' in the United States." *Proceedings of the Eighth Annual Conference of the Children's Literature Association,* University of Minnesota, March 1981, 106–18.

Zipes, Jack. 1979a. "Who's Afraid of the Brothers Grimm?" *Lion and the Unicorn* 3:4–57.

———. 1979b. *Breaking the Magic Spell.* Austin: University of Texas Press.

———. 1979c. "On the Use and Abuse of Folk and Fairy Tales with Children." *Proceedings of the Fifth Annual Conference of the Children's Literature Association,* Harvard University, March 1978, 113–22.

———. 1983. *The Trials and Tribulations of Little Red Riding Hood: Versions of the Tale in Sociocultural Context.* South Hadley, Mass.: Bergin and Garvey, Ltd.

Index

INDEX

Mercure Galant, 10
Mesilat ha-Limud (Ben-Zeev), 150, 153
Mogridge, George, 171
More, Hanna, 170
Morrissey, Thomas J., 124
Mother Goose, 173, 175

Nancy Drew series, 94, 95–96, 100, 102, 103, 104, 105, 106, 107, 110, 114, 179. *See also* Keene, Carolyn
Neuberg, Victor E., 163, 175
Newbery, Elizabeth, 174
Newbery, John, 74, 140, 145, 166–69
North, Sterling: *Rascal*, 144
The Nursery Alice (Carroll), 72

O'Dell, Scott, 40
O'Hara, Mary: *My Friend Flicka*, 144
Opie, Iona, 39
Opie, Peter, 39
Ovid: *Metamorphosis*, 160

Paget, Rev. F. E., *The Hope of the Katzekopfs*, 76
Peachey, Caroline, 76
Perrault, Charles, 9–16, 17–32 *passim*, 175; "Little Red Riding Hood," 8, 9–16, 19, 23, 24, 25, 26, 30; *Histoires ou Contes du temps passé*, 9–12, 19, 76; *La Cabinet des Fées*, 10; *La Marquise de Salusses ou la Patience de Griselidis*, 10; *Les Souhaits ridicules*, 10; *La Belle au Bois Dormant (Sleeping Beauty)*, 11;

L'Histoire de la Marquise-Marquis de Banneville, 11; editions of works, 32
Perry, Menakhem, 46
Pestalozzi, Johann Heinrich, 148n
Philanthropinismus, 148, 149
Pilkington, Mary: *The Renowned History of Primrose Prettyface*, 167
Poet Jests, or Mirth in Abundance, 161
Pollock, Linda A., 5
Popular Tales from the Norse, 76
Prince of Troy, 161

Rasselas, 163
Reynard the Fox, 139, 142, 160, 166
Robin Hood, 161
Robinson Crusoe (Defoe), 43, 112, 115–16, 123, 129, 139, 161, 179; translation of, 126–28; Zamoshch Hebrew translation of, 128, 129
Robinson der Jüngere (Defoe; trans. Campe), 127, 154, 155
Robinsonnades, 116n, 127, 154
Roderic Random, 162
Rölleke, Heinz, 20
Rousseau, Jean Jacques, 139, 140, 141; pedagogical system, 127; *Émile*, 154
Ruskin, John: *The King of the Golden River*, 76–77
Russell, Bertrand, 81

Satenof, Isaak: *Mišle Asaf*, 156
Scherf, Walter, 37
Schiller, Friedrich, 153
Scriptures: and children's reading, 137, 139, 151